C

PARANORMAL
PETERSBURG

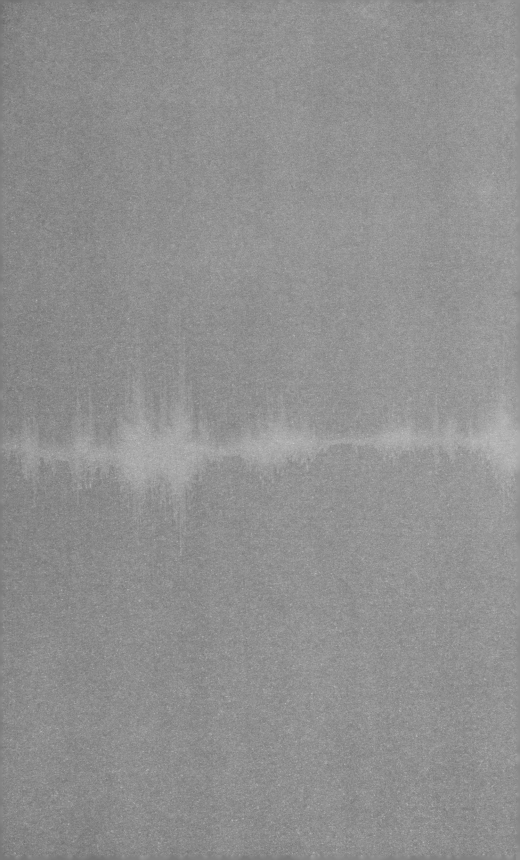

PARANORMAL
PETERSBURG
VIRGINIA & THE TRI-CITIES AREA

Pamela K. Kinney

Schiffer Publishing Ltd

4880 Lower Valley Road • Atglen, PA 19310

Other Schiffer Books by the Author:

Haunted Richmond, 978-0-7643-2712-4
Haunted Richmond II, 978-0-7643-3964-6
Haunted Virginia: Legends, Myths, and True Tales, 978-0-7643-3281-4
Virginia's Haunted Historic Triangle, Williamsburg, Yorktown, Jamestown,
& Other Haunted Locations, 978-0-7643-3746-8

Designed by John P. Cheek
Cover design by Matt Goodman
Type set in Akzidenz-Grotesk BQ/Scala

ISBN: 978-0-7643-4942-3
Printed in China

Published by Schiffer Publishing, Ltd.
4880 Lower Valley Road
Atglen, PA 19310
Phone: (610) 593-1777; Fax: (610) 593-2002
E-mail: Info@schifferbooks.com

For our complete selection of fine books on this and related subjects, please visit our website at www.schifferbooks.com. You may also write for a free catalog.

This book may be purchased from the publisher. Please try your bookstore first.

We are always looking for people to write books on new and related subjects. If you have an idea for a book, please contact us at proposals@schifferbooks.com.

Schiffer Publishing's titles are available at special discounts for bulk purchases for sales promotions or premiums. Special editions, including personalized covers, corporate imprints, and excerpts can be created in large quantities for special needs. For more information, contact the publisher.

I dedicate this book to the memory of author L.B. Taylor Jr., who passed away, joining the ranks of ghosts that he wrote about in his Virginia ghost books.

I'm also adding a special dedication to my husband, Bill, for coming with me to some of these places and being behind my writing about them — 100 per cent. You're my hero.

Contents

Introduction

IN CULTURE AFTER CULTURE, PEOPLE BELIEVE THAT THE
SOUL LIVES ON AFTER DEATH, THAT RITUALS CAN CHANGE
THE PHYSICAL WORLD AND DIVINE THE TRUTH, AND THAT
ILLNESS AND MISFORTUNE ARE CAUSED AND ALLEVIATED
BY SPIRITS, GHOSTS, SAINTS...AND GODS.

—STEVEN PINKER

South of Richmond, down I-95, lies the city of Petersburg. It is surrounded by Colonial Heights, Hopewell, Prince George, Dinwiddie, with Chester and Ettrick-Matoaca of Chesterfield County nearby.

In 1645, Fort Henry was established for the defense of the inhabitants on the south side of the James River. Fort Henry's commander and owner, Abraham Wood, rose to the rank of major general of the militia, participated in Indian relations, revised laws of the colony, and led expeditions to the south and west. From 1638 to 1675, Fort Henry became a center of trade and exploration.

Peter Jones succeeded Abraham Wood as leader in the area in 1675. He married Abraham Wood's daughter, Margaret, and continued the trade established by Wood. He took charge of Fort Henry and established his own trading post. Local tradition indicates that Petersburg may have been named for Peter Jones; however, there is no documentation to prove that.

Colonel William Byrd II led an expedition in 1733 to land near the Virginia-North Carolina border. He laid the foundation of two towns, Richmond and "Petersburg," during this expedition.

Separate in the beginning, the towns of Petersburg and Blandford incorporated in 1748, followed by the town of Pocahontas in 1752. The towns of Petersburg, Blandford, and Pocahontas, along with the suburbs of Ravenscroft and Bollingbrook, all became one town called Petersburg. Petersburg elected John Banister as its first mayor in 1781. As you will read later, he is still a presence around Petersburg.

The Petersburg branch of Farmer's Bank of Virginia opened in 1812 in rented quarters in an unknown location that burned down in 1815. The bank operated from its 1817 building on Bollingbrook Street, closing after the Civil War. The Fort Henry branch of the Association for the Preservation of Virginia Antiquities restored the building after acquiring it in 1963. Today, the Siege Museum inhabits it. Bollingbrook Street became the first paved street for the city in 1813. The Virginia Assembly incorporated Petersburg as Virginia's third city in 1850. The South Side Railroad Station was built in 1854 and is the oldest railroad station in Virginia. It is also the site where Robert E. Lee began his retreat to Appomattox. The Ladies Memorial Association held Petersburg's first Memorial Day celebration at Blandford Cemetery on June 9, 1866. Wilkerson Funeral Home opened in 1874, and it remains the longest operating black-owned business in Petersburg. Peabody High School, one of the first African-American high schools in Virginia, was also built at this time. In 1882, Virginia Normal and Collegiate Institute was established; however, it is now Virginia State University. Petersburg adopted a city manager form of government in 1820.

Much of Petersburg is connected to Prince George and Dinwiddie Counties. With so much history, no doubt the paranormal saturates the area as well. Petersburg is full of history, beginning from 1864 and stretching forward to present day. Petersburg not only has historical context, it also has a significant ghostly influence as well.

Hopewell separated from Prince George County and Colonial Heights parted from Chesterfield County. All are interlocked, one way or another. Much of the history is too.

Equipment and Procedures for Investigating

In the following chapters I will be talking about the equipment I use for investigating the paranormal. When someone first starts investigating with a group, they often just use a digital camera and maybe a pad of paper and a pen to write down things. Plus a good flashlight is always a smart thing to have on hand. Then there are extra batteries, as the spirits suck the power out of them to help them manifest. This was all I used when researching my first book, *Haunted Richmond, Virginia*.

Digital Recorder

The next piece of equipment I bought was a digital recorder. This helped me get electronic voice phenomena (EVPs). This recorder is small and easy to carry. When using audio recorders on investigations, be sure to state the location, time of investigation, and participating investigators' names. When recording the names of each investigator, it would be wise to have each individual present state their own names, which will make it easier for distinction amongst voices heard on the recording during review. I also use my recorder for interviews, as it makes it easy to go back over and over what someone said to me when I interviewed them.

EMF Meter

I started using an electromagnetic field meter/detector (EMF) while researching my third book, *Virginia's Haunted Historic Triangle: Williamsburg, Yorktown, Jamestown, and Other Haunted Locations*. With this instrument, it is possible to locate and track energy sources—even communicate with a spirit and have them answer you back when you ask them to flash lights shown on the unit. The meter detects fluctuations in electromagnetic fields and low-strength, moving EMF fields that have no source. It is a common theory that spirits disrupt this field in such a way that you can tell one is present by higher-than-normal readings with this meter. Before I use the EMF as a ghost research tool, I walk around the area and take initial readings around energy sources such as light poles or electrical outlets to be sure of the readings I receive while scanning the area during the investigation. When using the EMF as a tracking device, look for fluctuations of 2.0 to 7.0; this usually indicates spirit presence. Anything higher or lower normally has a natural source. I was on the fence with this tool until I actually had a spirit flash a number of lights when I told it how many to flash.

Pendulum and Dowsing Rods

I also use the pendulum and dowsing rods. Not scientific, but still, if you are psychic (and honestly, you have to be even a little bit for the other equipment to work), then these can be useful. A pendulum is usually a small, heavy object—like a stone, a crystal, or even a piece of metal—suspended from a cord, ribbon, or chain. A necklace can be ideal for this. Someone (like me) holds the cord, ribbon, or chain so the heavy object can swing freely. I ask mostly yes or no questions and suggest that answers be given by movement of the object either back and forth or in a circle to give me those answers. I tell the spirits that I will not move my arm or hand; they have to make the pendulum move.

Dowsing rods are made of willow or hazel. These divining rods were used to find water and even used by those who work with sewer departments to locate sewers. They can be used in paranormal investigating, too, as a form of communication tool. Another type of dowsing or witching rod is one using two brass "L"-shaped wire rods (commonly made of brazing or welding rod, but glass or plastic have also been accepted) that are to be held one in each hand. The ones I used are metal and I bought them at the gift shop at the Ferry Plantation House in Virginia Beach, Virginia.

The Ovilus

Now I do not own an Ovilus but my friend, Carol Smith, does. The Ovilus modulates the energy changes into audible speech using a synthesizer chip, an extensive English word dictionary, and a function that phonetically sounds out words. The voice that throws out the word sounds robotic to me. Most of the time, the words do not seem to fit anything; then again, there are those times it makes a sentence or throws out a word that is connected to the investigation.

Laser Grid

The laser grid is another piece of equipment I have used at some investigations for this book, filming *Paranormal World Seekers*, or just a regular investigation. The high powered laser emits a grid of green dots useful for detecting shadows or general visual disturbances during an investigation. You can adjust the size and shape of the stars by turning the adjustable lens. Detach the lens and it will function as a high powered laser pointer. So you can see what they do, I found this demonstration on Youtube: www.youtube.com/watch?v=_Sw35W1y_bA.

Ghost Box

I use the "ghost box," or "Frank's Box," (created by Frank Sumption) as it is also called. It is used to contact spirits through the use of radio frequency (scanning mode) of a radio modified to act as a medium for direct communication. In other words, ghosts use the white noise to talk to you.

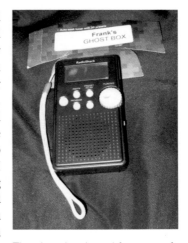

I've learned to figure what sounds provided are just from radio stations and those that are not—by trial and error. I do think you have to be psychic in some way to use it effectively. I also use my recorder to record the session using the box for later listening to be sure what I heard was true spirit communication or even to get a word I didn't realize initially in real time. I even ask the spirits to say something to me to prove it really is them. Most of the time, like any of the equipment I use, that doesn't mean I will

The ghost box I used for many of the investigations in this book.

get answers right away, or they will come in rapid succession. Sometimes there is nothing and after ten minutes of nothing, it is best to move on.

In Action

So that you can actually see me in action, using my ghost box and even the EMF meter and recorder, following is the link to the first episode of *Paranormal World Seekers*, filmed by my co-producer, Mark Layne of AVA Productions: www.youtube.com/watch?v=URSIO9hhZTI (It is also available on DVD.)

I hope this will help those of you who might be interested in the varied types of equipment I (and other investigators) use on paranormal investigations. When I mention them in the chapters of the book this explanation should make it easier to understand there are times I might get a lot of information and other times, nothing at all or just an answer or two. Nothing is an exact science and after all, the paranormal is still unknown territory.

So come check out the phantoms that still occupy Petersburg, Colonial Heights, Hopewell, Prince George County, Dinwiddie County, and even nearby Ettrick-Matoaca, Enon, and Chester. They are just *dying* to meet you.

PETERSBURG

HISTORY WITH ITS FLICKERING LAMP STUMBLES ALONG
THE TRAIL OF THE PAST, TRYING TO RECONSTRUCT
ITS SCENES, TO REVIVE ITS ECHOES, AND KINDLE
WITH PALE GLEAMS THE PASSION OF FORMER DAYS.
—WINSTON CHURCHILL

There are three centuries of architectural heritage in seven national historic districts along the Appomattox River Heritage Trail. The town is rich in Civil War history after engaging in a several months-long siege before Robert E. Lee left for Sailor's Creek and the last battle of the War Between the States.

It also has a rich African-American history. This town had the oldest free black community in the United States, settling Pocahontas Island—and it is still there today. It is a peninsula on the north side of the Appomattox River within the limits of Petersburg. Petersburg's first enslaved African-Americans were brought here in 1732 to work in John Bolling's tobacco warehouses. Bolling owned haunted Centre Hill Mansion (mentioned in another chapter). It was subdivided and named Wittontown in 1750, but was renamed Pocahontas when it became a town in 1752. It became part of Petersburg in 1784. Most of Petersburg's 310 free blacks probably resided in this integrated neighborhood by the 1800s, including John Jarrett and John Updike, who earned their livings as boatmen, fishermen and watermen. Pocahontas Island is listed on the National Register of Historic Places.

In 1973, Hermanze E. Fauntleroy Jr. became Petersburg's first black mayor. Florence Farley became the first black woman to serve on the Petersburg City Council in 1973. In 1984, she became Petersburg's first black woman mayor.

Richard A. Stewart, the unofficial "mayor" of Pocahontas Island, was born on the sixty-six-acre island in 1943 and purchased an eighteenth-century house in 2002. He collected and amassed artifacts related to black and Civil War history. Founding the Pocahontas Island Black History Museum, he opened it in 2003. (You can visit, but call first for an appointment as hours may vary. The phone number is 804-861-8889. Find out more at www.pocahontasislandmuseum.com.)

The Revolutionary War is connected to Petersburg. There was a 233rd anniversary of the reenactment of the 1781 Battle of Petersburg at Battersea April 19-20, 2014. (I attended on Easter Sunday, April 20, 2014). While Battersea is not the actual site of the 1781 battlefield, it was utilized by the British troops when they occupied the town in May of 1781. Battersea was the home of Colonel John Banister, the first mayor of Petersburg and a signer of the Articles of Confederation.

Due to Petersburg Volunteers fighting at the Siege of Fort Megis on May 5, 1781, during the War of 1812, the city, named by President James Madison, was "Cockade of the Union" (or "Cockade City," in honor of the cockades the Volunteers wore on their caps).

Petersburg suffered the Great Fire on July 16, 1815. More than 350 buildings were destroyed with an estimated $3,000,000 in damage. After that, Petersburg residents began building using brick. Between 1815 and 1817, Petersburg saw the emergence of approximately 300 brick buildings.

The Richmond-Petersburg Campaign or the Siege, was a series of nine offensives by the Union forces against the Confederates defending Petersburg and Richmond, Virginia. The Siege of Petersburg happened between June 9, 1864 and March 25, 1865. Upwards of 50,000 Union soldiers and 32,000 Confederates died during this time. Food was in short supply; corn became "coffee," and blackberry leaves "tea." A chicken cost $50. Beginning after the unsuccessful attack of the city of Petersburg by Ulysses Grant, construction trenches were erected around the eastern portion of Richmond to the outskirts of Petersburg. The city was a major supply hub to the Confederate army led by Robert E. Lee, who finally abandoned the city in 1865 and retreated , leading to his ultimate surrender at Appomattox Courthouse. The Siege of Petersburg was an early example of trench warfare used extensively in World War I.

Three Places in Old Towne Petersburg

The South Side Railroad Depot served the South Side Railroad line and was the last railroad operating during the Siege of Petersburg. When Union troops severed the rail line, it ensured the surrender of Petersburg and Richmond. After the war, South Side Depot became a nexus of political development for Virginia. William Mahone, a former Confederate hero-turned-readjuster had his office on its second floor. The Readjuster Party was formed as a biracial coalition party partaking of many great accomplishments, such as the establishment of the Virginia Normal and Collegiate Institute (now Virginia State University).

The South Side Railroad Depot.

Petersburg's courthouse was built between 1837 and 1839 and served as the Confederate headquarters during the Siege of Petersburg. Volunteers gathered in its square to enlist on April 20, 1861. When its bell sounded on June 9, 1864, local militia met the advancing Union cavalry. Soldiers from both sides could see the courthouse clock from the trenches during the siege, and they set their timepieces by it. The clock tower was a favorite target of Union artillerists, who poured an estimated 20,000 shells into the city. When Petersburg fell on April 3, 1865, a Union flag was raised to its top.

Petersburg Courthouse. It was a prominent landmark during the Siege of Petersburg in the Civil War.

At **9 East Old Street**, a unique octagonal building was constructed in the late 1870s on a site given to the city in 1806 by the Bolling family. The land had long been used as a market, and the current building is only the most recent of four that were built on the site, the earliest dating back to 1787. The building has been used as a market, a restaurant, and, most recently, a setting for Steven Spielberg's film *Lincoln* and the AMC television series *Turn*.

Today, Petersburg is a city of history dressed in the latest fashions, but its historical beginnings still show beneath its skirts. There is New Millennium Movie Studios not far from Richard Bland College. I remember passing the fenced studios as I drove to college (I'd attended for a couple of years to major in theatre.). Films like *The Contender* shot interiors at New Millennium and employed its Oval Office and its White House exterior. The movie, based on Stephen King's novel *Hearts in Atlantis* (I worked on set as a principal extra!) shot some pieces on the studios' soundstage.

Its Revolutionary War and Civil War history are strongly entrenched. One can tour Blandford Church and Cemetery where cannon balls have taken a piece from a gravestone, the nearby Civil War battlefields, Siege Museum, and much more. Its historical downtown has charming restaurants, shops, and antiques. There is something for every member of the family. Most of all, Petersburg is a place where one can have a spirited time—and I am not talking about alcohol. I am talking ghosts. After all, the city in the historical downtown section has a ghost tour in the fall, and it's not shy about talking about its haunts.

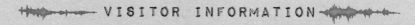

VISITOR INFORMATION

South Side Railroad Depot
Rock and River Streets
Petersburg, VA. 23803
www.preservationpetersburg.org/explore_southside_depot.html

This depot is no longer in use and only an empty building sits there now.

A good website to research places would be at www.petersburgva.gov. You will find maps, information about Petersburg Transit, the city's museums, places to stay or dine, and the area's attractions.

But most of all, Petersburg has the dead waiting for you.

Hiram Haines Coffee and Ale House

THE BOUNDARIES WHICH DIVIDE LIFE FROM DEATH ARE
AT BEST SHADOWY AND VAGUE. WHO SHALL SAY WHERE
THE ONE ENDS, AND WHERE THE OTHER BEGINS?
                              —EDGAR ALLAN POE

Hiram Haines Coffee and Ale House.

Hiram Haines Coffee and Ale House in the Old Towne section of Petersburg has more than coffee, ale, wine, and good food to offer. The restaurant is haunted, too.

It was constructed in 1814 by Richard Hannon, who owned nearby Powhatton Plantation. Run by French émigré Richard Rambaut and his wife Countess Elise de Rochefoucauld, it became a luxury hotel. When the market crashed in 1827, the legend tells that Rambaut committed suicide in the place, taking poison after he wrote a letter to his wife.

The next to acquire the building was Hiram Haines, a local poet and newspaper editor of the *American Constellation* in Petersburg. He turned it into Hiram Haines Coffee and Ale House. He moved his wife and six children next door to No. 16. This would be the building in back of the coffee house. The main level was used for newspaper offices.

An interesting thing about Haines was that he played an important role in Edgar Allan Poe's life. No one can pinpoint when both men became friends,

Edgar Allan Poe is the prevailing theme at the restaurant.

but Haines's wife was the daughter of a wealthy Richmond merchant, and she had known Poe as a child. It was said that Poe and Haines' wife looked like brother and sister, at least by the Haines' family records. When General Lafayette visited Richmond in 1824, there happened to be a young cadet at Burkes Academy: Lieutenant Edgar Allan Poe. Poe led his "Richmond Junior Volunteers" in saluting a Revolutionary War hero with swords drawn. The next day, Lafayette traveled twenty miles south to Petersburg where twenty-two-year-old Hiram Haines kicked off the general's visit with a poem of welcome at Niblo's Tavern.

Hiram Haines Coffee and Ale House became the spot for poets, journalists, and intellectuals to gather in 1829. These cafes/taverns were politically provocative and intellectually charged dens frequented by eminent scholars and libertines. They were very unlike what we think of coffee shops today. On the upper floors, the rooms surpassed anything in Richmond. Poe first visited the tavern when he was with the *Southern Messenger* in Richmond and the two men's friendship grew during Poe's years at the publisher. When Poe married his cousin, Virginia Clemm, Haines convinced the couple to honeymoon in Petersburg, and they stayed in rooms on the second floor above the tavern. One local historian wrote in her book that the Poes were wined and dined for two weeks.

The coffee house/restorative operated from 1829 until late in 1836. When Haines began to have financial problems, he sold the building. Dying of bilious pleurisy in 1841, his grave, along with his wife's, is in Blandford Cemetery.

It was in 2010 when Hiram Haines Shop and Ale House reopened, this time by Jeffrey Abugel.

Interview with Jeffrey Abugel

On Thursday, December 3, 2013, I drove to meet with Jeff Abugel to interview him about his haunted restaurant. Even though we weren't meeting until 2 p.m. for the interview and my investigation of the building afterwards, I left early to check out the other haunted locations in the area. Just as I parked in the public parking lot at the corner of E. Old and N. Sycamore Streets, it began to rain. The local news had said nothing about rain that day; in fact, the temperatures were in the low 70s, so I was very surprised. Not able to locate my umbrella, I stopped at Wabi Sabi to set up a future interview, then I walked over to the Petersburg Historical Society, to Old Street, then stopped at Blue Willow Tea Shop for some hot tea and scones—as well as to dry off. It was there that I learned that Blue Willow Tea Shop has some ghosts, too.

The rain stopped about an hour and half before I needed to be at Hiram Haines Coffee and Ale House. I looked up at the second floor window, where it appeared someone looked out the window to my far right. I found out later, that it was, in fact, a store dummy, like the ones used to display clothing. There is a legend that says on the anniversary of Virginia Clemm Poe's death, she can been seen staring out this same window. For anyone wanting to see if she joins the dummy at the window, she passed away from tuberculosis on January 30, 1847.

When the time came for the interview, I stepped inside Hiram Haines and saw Jeff Abugel in a booth with several other people. He asked if I would like a cup of coffee and led me to a table near the front door. After making sure his customers were comfortable in the restaurant, he took the seat across from me, and we began the interview.

My first question pertained to any experiences he'd had with the ghosts in the building. He related a story about a psychic who came to visit Hiram Haines. This psychic traveled around the country at people's behest. Jeff escorted the psychic to the second floor where he sensed a man, Richard Rambaut, pacing back and forth. Rambaut was thinking about a life and death situation to end his life; was this a residual haunting and not an intelligent haunting? A residual haunting is known in the paranormal field as a loop—where phantom images do something at certain times or dates over and over, but do not interact or answer questions—for example, those within a residual haunting do not respond during an EVP session—or it walks past you without any acknowledgment at all.

That was the only thing the psychic got from the second floor. When Jeff took him up to the third floor, though, the psychic went into a trance. He smiled and giggled. Then he turned to Abugel and laughed.

Jeff asked, "Why are you laughing at me?"

"I see you in long hair, like a hippie from 1960s."

The 1960s? Jeff thought that was odd, when he realized that maybe he meant the 1860s. The psychic confirmed this when he talked about wounded and ill Civil War soldiers being tended by a woman on the third floor. She acted as a nurse, leaving the room to bring back wet cloths to place over their brows. Another woman, her sister or a relative, told her she could move on, but though the soldiers disappeared, the spectral woman remained.

The psychic and Jeff headed back downstairs. The third floor had left the psychic feeling physically and emotionally drained. Jeff felt that there were other things the man never told him. When the psychic tried to go to the front door, he told Jeff it felt as if a wall of bone-chilling cold hovered between him and the exit. Jeff felt pretty sure that the visit happened during the summer, although he couldn't remember for sure. There would have been air conditioning on, but he hadn't felt that cold—not with customers coming in and out, bringing in the heat.

The next question I asked was, "Do you believe Edgar Allan Poe and his wife Virginia, or either of them, might still be hanging around?"

Jeff replied, "Beings this was the happiest two weeks of their lives, it could be likely."

I asked, "Do you think Hiram Haines is haunting the place?"

"From what I got to know about him, I doubt it. He was peace-loving, happy and, even though beset with financial problems and dying at a young age while his wife lived on, I don't think so. Reading his thoughts in his letters, I felt close to him. The letters seemed more like a contemporary man wrote them. I felt kindred to him, like he might be a father or relative, even like me."

Something struck me. I asked if he thought that maybe he could be a reincarnation of Haines.

"Maybe," he said. "That might explain why I can't get my mind off this place or him."

I asked if any of his customers or workers had seen or heard anything paranormal in nature. He told me that customers especially would feel something on the second floor walkway when they were in the Rue Morgue room of the restaurant. They explained it was a feeling like something watching them from the spot next to the barrel closest to the door. When they tried to take photographs with their cameras or smartphones, the electronics wouldn't work. When I used the ghost box and held an EVP session in the Rue Morgue later, my ghost box turned off four times. My camera *did* work that day in the Rue Morgue and the other two times I had been in the restaurant before. When customers took photos, they usually caught orbs or shadows in them. I caught a shadow back in September 2013—the Saturday before my birthday—when my husband took me to eat there. It was in the Rue Morgue—not up on the walkway, though.

Walkway Above the Rue Morgue

Other paranormal activity experienced were objects moving from their normal spots and found elsewhere; however, no one living admitted to moving them. Objects would also fly off the walls or shelves without notice. One time, a beer bottle just exploded. One waitress confided that she could feel something in the restaurant. There was an event and she couldn't find something she needed on a shelf in the kitchen and said out loud, "Really?" At that moment, something fell from a different shelf. "Really?" she asked again. She felt a shy, female spirit haunted the kitchen area.

I also inquired whether Jeff had anything occur in the building next door at River's Edge, where he and his wife conducted some of their business. He said the strangest thing happened: they found five or six bird skeletons frozen in standing positions—no feathers, flesh, skin, or organs, just the bones. It appeared they had been like that for a long time.

Walkway above the Rue Morgue.

The Investigation—Rue Morgue

I did both an EVP and ghost box session in the Rue Morgue before Bill and I took the Petersburg Ghost Tour on Friday, November 11, 2014. At one point, when I asked for a name, I heard what sounded like "Derek." Another was a "Yes," when I'd asked if any spirits were there.

For the investigation of the two upper floors, on December 3, Jeff took me to a closed door off the hallway, opposite the restrooms for the restaurant. It led into a back room filled with bookcases, a table, and some chairs. A staircase went up to the second floor. At the top of the stairs, I saw a door that opened to a walkway between the two buildings that allowed you to look down on the Rue Morgue. Also near the door, to the right, another staircase climbed up to the third floor. An ominous impression wafted from the shadows up there.

The opposite end of the landing led to the Poe honeymoon suite. At this point, Jeff told me he had to go back downstairs to attend to the cases of beer and ale that had just been delivered. I told him I would be fine.

Poe's Honeymoon Suite on the Second Floor

I walked into the sitting room of the suite and dropped my bag of paranormal investigating equipment and my purse on the old-fashioned couch. Two matching chairs stood on each side of the couch and an old-fashioned chest of drawers stood between the two windows that looked down onto the street, where you could see the Siege Museum. A fireplace loomed behind the couch and, across the room, a table stood against the wall. In the other room I found a bed; however, I doubted it was the original bed Poe and his bride shared. Back in the sitting room, I took note of a female mannequin, wearing skimpy underwear and a wedding veil, perched on the ledge of the window, and she appeared to be staring out. An old-fashioned typewriter with a pair of disembodied hands on the keys nestled against the far wall just behind her dangling feet. The horror writer in me expected them to begin typing at any minute.

The typewriter with the disembodied hands on the floor.

I took some pictures with my camera, then employed my pendulum to see if anyone or anything was there and asked if they would swing it back and forth. Not moving my arm or hand—as I told them, *they* had to do it—the pendulum went immediately into a heavy swing. After I thanked them and asked them to stop, it came to a standstill. Did that mean Poe and Virginia were there? Or

The sitting room used by Poe and his bride during their honeymoon.

The bedroom used for Poe's and Virginia's honeymoon.

could it be the first owner, Richard Rambaut, the man the psychic sensed? Maybe Hiram himself or even someone else?

Next, I took out the recorder, turned it on, and began an EVP session. Nothing was noted from the regular EVP session on the second floor when I listened to it later at home, except when I knocked on the table and asked, "Can you do a knock like that?" I did not hear it live when I was present in the house; but on the recording, I heard two knocks exactly like mine, lighter and from elsewhere in the room.

When I used the ghost box for a session, I got interesting results. I'd asked if Edgar Allan Poe or his wife Virginia were in the room with me; I didn't receive an answer. Maybe they had been so happy honeymooning here, they felt no reason to return to the building to haunt it. And to be honest, I did not sense Poe at all that day.

"Is there anyone else with me?" I asked.

A man's voice came across the ghost box. "Yes."

"Richard Rambaut, are you here?"

"Yes."

"Can you speak in French to me, Richard, to prove it is you."

"Oui."

"Why are you haunting this building? Can you tell me?"

"No."

Either he knew why and did not want to tell me, or he really had no idea why. Maybe, since he'd committed suicide, this caused the doors to the other side to remain closed to him.

I asked, "Can you give me the date of your death?"

There was an answer, but too low to hear. I asked for the date of the spirit's death again and I heard a partial, "18—"

Then I heard a partial word, sounding like "threat..." The rest cut off or the spirit couldn't get the balance of it out.

Was this still Richard? Perhaps another spirit? Had he been threatened, or was he threatening me?

I asked if the spirit that had said the name Derek, down in the Rue Morgue, was on the second floor with me. I got an answer to this question with "Yes." Who was Derek? I wanted to know, but received no answer.

I asked if Haines was there. Again, I received no answer.

I asked what the spirits thought of Jeff, who now owned the building, or any of the workers downstairs. Nothing.

Then another word popped out. "Fort." Civil War maybe? I asked, but no one answered me. Maybe this was from a Confederate soldier who had been hospitalized in the building during the Siege.

I left the room to snap more pictures and a "Hello" came out from my box that I'd left with the recorder back in the sitting room, so I didn't hear it until I listened to the recording at home. When I drew closer to the room a few minutes later, I heard a man's voice loud and clear, "Hello!"

I called out, "Hello?"

No one answered me. It was on my recording, but it did not sound as if it came from my ghost box. Had one of the spirits missed me? Richard? The Derek person?

I used my EMF meter, hoping the ghosts would register on the dial as well, but nothing happened. Finally, after a few more pictures shot in the sitting room (one of the photos of the fireplace had a shadow in it, and yet

Shadow on fireplace in the sitting room in Poe's honeymoon suite.

no shadows were in the picture before or afterwards), I grabbed my flashlight, EMF meter, recorder, and ghost box, and slung the camera around my neck.

Third Floor

I climbed the steps to the third floor. A feeling of oppression overcame me as I stepped onto the landing. I am sure some of it came from the phantoms of the Civil War soldiers, as this floor had been used for a hospital during the Siege. Some of it, though, I attribute to the obvious original lead-based paint on the wall and the dust. Boxes of stuff filled the rooms. I assumed all of it came from the ovens in the other building behind the eatery that Jeff discovered. The place that had been Hiram Haines' home when he was alive.

My EMF meter gave me nothing, so I shut it off and turned on my

The stairs leading up to the third floor.

recorder for an EVP session. At first, I got nothing—no voices and no sounds. I switched on the ghost box and it shut off three times. The recorder shut off once. Had the ghosts *physically* done this, or was it from them sucking the energy from the batteries as they tried to manifest?

I wandered around and asked questions. A woman's voice told me her name was Ann. Men's voices spouted off various names. (Remember that

Whose face is on the window pane on the third floor?

psychic who said he thought the men left—looks like they hadn't.) I took photos with my camera. When I was done, I sauntered down the stairs to the landing, using my ghost box and recording, while taking some photographs. The same woman's voice who told me her name was Ann came across the ghost box, "Oh, will you please stop it?" That's when I knew it was time for me to quit and head back downstairs. I thought that the spirits' patience might be at an end, and I did not want to chance being pushed down the steps. You never know what spirits may try when they are angry.

After my investigation, I stopped to say goodbye to Jeff before heading home. While I had been upstairs, a friend of Jeff's dropped by with a first-edition copy of the *Southern Messenger* that Poe worked on. He knew Jeff had been searching for it to add to his Poe collection. He only charged him what he paid for it: $30. Jeff felt that maybe my being there, brought him luck in getting this.

In one photo that I took on the third floor of two windows overlooking the Rue Morgue, you can see a face in the second pane from the bottom of the window, to the left. I thought, *Poe?* But Poe never answered that he was there in spirit on either floor. There is no picture of Poe or any other face hanging on the Rue Morgue walls—not that high up. I didn't notice a face in the window panes on any of the two upper floors. After examining the photos, I thought again, "Is it Poe? Or someone else?" When I sent it to Jeff, he said it looked like a young Poe. (How weird is that?) Later, someone pointed out that many young men in the nineteenth century had their hair arranged like Poe's. It was the fashion of the times. And contrary to what the film *Lincoln* made claim to, there were men during the Civil War time who did not sport beards or mustaches. Besides, the soldiers on the third floor had a nurse, who could have shaved their faces. All I know is, Poe never answered me. That's not to say he wasn't there, I just don't have proof.

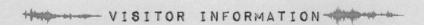

VISITOR INFORMATION

Hiram Haines Coffee and Ale House
12 West Bank Street
Petersburg, Virginia 23803
www.riversedgeinteriors.com/poepage1.htm

This business has closed and is for sale at the time of this printing.

Wabi Sabi

NOW IT IS THE TIME OF NIGHT
THAT THE GRAVES, ALL GAPING WIDE,
EVERY ONE LETS FORTH HIS SPRITE
IN THE CHURCH-WAY PATHS TO GLIDE.

—WILLIAM SHAKESPEARE

Wabi Sabi.

Wabi Sabi at 29 Bollingbrook Street has more than good food, drinks, and a good time; it also has ghosts. Its paranormal activity comes from the varied past of the building. Built in 1815–1816, the building housed a brothel and was known as the Nathaniel Friend House. It is a three-and-one-half-story, six bay, Federal-style, brick commercial/residential building with a rear annex that incorporates the original kitchen and smokehouse.

The house was built by Nathaniel Friend Jr., who served as the mayor of Petersburg in 1812–1813 and was also a wealthy import-export merchant. He purchased the corner at Bollingbrook Street and Market Lane (now Cockade Alley) for $7,000 from Robert Bolling and William Haxall in 1815. Nathaniel Friend Jr. was one of seven children born to Nathaniel Friend (1741–1795) and Sally Walthal (1747–1795) in Chesterfield County. Around 1812, he married Elizabeth Gilliam, daughter of William Gilliam and Christian Epps of City Point Farm. He had three children. In addition to his holdings in Petersburg, Friend Jr. owned a plantation known as "White Hill," which he purchased from John Gilliam in 1798. After the great fire of 1815, many square blocks of earlier wooden-frame buildings burned down in the old Petersburg area, causing Nathaniel to erect three new brick buildings. Nathaniel Friend Building was listed in the National Register of Historic Places in 1976.

Sprenkle and Company completed a careful restoration of the entire three-story building for both commercial and residential use. They worked to incorporate as much of the structural history of the building into the renovation as possible. Original support beams were removed and reused wherever possible over doorways and in the basement. The ground floors were renovated for commercial use as a restaurant, retail store, therapeutic massage center, and a sushi restaurant. The second story became a local art gallery that showcased a range of artists from Richmond and Petersburg. The third floor involved building several two-level residential condominiums, complete with original arched windows and reclaimed wood floors.

People had experiences in the apartments on the floors above Wabi Sabi. DJ Payne, the owner of Wabi Sabi, told me that when he stayed in his nephew's apartment upstairs one time, he had his own experience. He was getting ready for work one morning, when the toilet in the bathroom flushed, even though no one was in the apartment but him. He thought, *Ah, Donny must be home.* Going to investigate, he found no one else in any of the rooms. His next thought: *Wait a moment, Donny's still in California.* It was then he realized that a ghost must be present.

The first time he took over the restaurant, Payne went downstairs to check the rooms. Today, the area has a bar with a kitchen behind it. There is no fireplace presently; however, there was one when DJ got the place. He'd stood with his back to it when a feeling overcame him of being watched. Turning, he saw a Confederate soldier standing next to him. The soldier appeared to be warming his bottom at the fireplace—except there was no fire. He immediately noticed that the spirit was African-American and then the ghost vanished after being seen.

DJ never mentioned the skin color of the ghost he saw, just that he had seen it. But one of his workers, Brandon, was at the bar and said, "You saw the black Confederate soldier downstairs, didn't you?" DJ felt flustered and replied that he hadn't mentioned it because he was from up north and never knew there were black Confederate soldiers in the Civil War. He thought people might be offended if he said anything about the phantom's skin color, too. (This was the first time that I'd found out there were black Confederates myself.)

On Monday, December 9, 2013, I parked in the same area where I had during the Hiram Haines Coffee and Ale House's tour. I turned the corner at Wabi Sabi and entered by the right-side door. I told an employee I was there to see the owner, so he went to find DJ and left me to check my camera. A feeling came over me at the back of my neck like someone was watching me. I whipped around and saw stairs going down into darkness. I snapped a picture and took another as the batteries died; however, in my viewfinder, it looked like a shadow parting from the darkness and rushing up the stairs at me.

The room downstairs haunted by the black Confederate ghost.

I grabbed a container full of batteries to insert new ones in the camera and quickly took more pictures of the darkened stairs, all while my hair continued to stand on end.

Shortly thereafter, DJ joined me and we talked about the history of the building. He led me downstairs to begin my investigation, and I started with an EVP session. After he went back upstairs, I turned on the ghost box.

"I've heard there is a child here. Can you tell me your name?"

"Philip." (It sounded like *Phil...ip.*)

I asked the child spirit, "Do you miss your parents? Are you an orphan? Did you work here?"

A woman's voice came over the ghost box, so I asked, "What is your name?" I thought I heard the woman reply: "Bree."

"Is it getting cold?"

Woman: "I'm warm."

"Philip, see my earrings?"

Child's voice: "Snowman." (I was wearing snowmen earrings at that time.)

"I've heard there is a Confederate soldier here. You can talk to me."

Man's voice: "Sure."

"To the child, Philip, I have a ball in my pack upstairs. Would you like me to get it?"

Child (sounding excited and loud): "Ball!"

I asked a few more questions, but didn't receive any answers. Finally when I asked, "How many spirits are with me here?"

I thought I heard "three" from the man. I asked, "Are the changes good?" after telling them that things had changed since their time, but neither the adult male or female ghosts answered.

The stairs that led down to the haunted room.

Close-up of the face of the black Confederate soldier peeking through the glass of the patio door. I got him like this in two consecutive photographs.

The child did, though. "No."

I asked, "To the black soldier here, what is your name?"

I heard a male voice say something, but the words were very low, so I am not sure he said his name or whether he replied with something else.

Me: "Why did you fight for the South?"

Man: "No."

Me: "Are you a free man? Or did you have a master?"

Man: "Free."

Did he mean free as in he was free and chose to join the Southern Army or was he a slave forced to become a Confederate and lied?

Me: "Black people are free today. Have you been upstairs and seen the black woman who works there?"

Man: "Yes."

Me: "She works for pay, so everything is much different now."

I heard footsteps coming downstairs and saw it was DJ.

Me: "Can you say hello to DJ?"

Man: "Hello."

Woman: "No."

The child said nothing.

They didn't say another word after that. I took some more photos, and in two of them, I saw the soldier peeking through the glass of the glass door. You could see his face and the gray Confederate private's cap perched on his head.

Whether phantoms of black Confederate soldiers, prostitutes, or children, you never know who you might be sharing a meal with at Wabi Sabi.

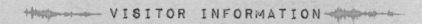

VISITOR INFORMATION

Wabi Sabi
29 Bollingbrook Street
Petersburg, VA 23803
804-862-1365
www.eatwabisabi.com

Open seven days a week. Its hours are Sunday/Monday/Tuesday from 11 a.m. to 9 p.m., Wednesday/Thursday from 11 a.m. to 12:30 a.m., and Friday/Saturday from 11 a.m. to 1.30 a.m.

Blue Willow Tea Room

MY HOUR FOR TEA IS HALF-PAST FIVE, AND MY BUTTERED
TOAST WAITS FOR NOBODY.

—WILKIE COLLINS

Blue Willow Tea Room.

There is nothing nicer than stopping at a tea room and dining on scones with Devonshire cream and blueberry jam, while enjoying hot tea—especially after a heavy downpour. You think of ladies in big hats, ceramic pots full of tea, and cucumber sandwiches. But you never think of ghosts, not in a million years. But the Blue Willow Tea Room at 104 West Old Street has more than charm and many delicious flavors of tea; it has a ghost upstairs. (My investigation would later reveal that more than one spirit haunted the floors above the tea room.)

Adjacent to Penniston's Alley Antiques and Collectibles, where old treasures were sold, the tea room charmed me. It was here that the film crew and extras of Steven Spielberg's *Lincoln* warmed up with soup and hot tea while filming, and several antique items were purchased or loaned for set props. The waitress told me that the owner researched English tea rooms, and this one was the closest to being like an English tea room. The scones were delightful and the tea warming. When I told the waitress I was investigating some places that held paranormal activity, she told me that there was a ghost upstairs.

Learning this, I talked to owner Sid Scott and managed to set a time to come by to not only interview him, but to investigate the floors above.

Inside the Blue Willow Tea Room.

Second-Floor Investigation

I returned on December 19, 2014, in the afternoon, when the place would be empty of customers. Sid Scott led me upstairs to the second floor and into one room on the right side of the building. He told me someone had said they had seen a man by a small table in the middle of the room.

The table where someone had seen a male spirit, possibly the first mayor of Petersburg. Taken on the second floor.

When I asked, "Any spirit with us?" a light flashed on my EMF meter.

I had my recorder on, but did not get any EVP on the second floor. Most of what I got that day came through the ghost box, but I did get one straight EVP when I was changing the batteries in my camera while on the third floor, just before we had headed back downstairs at the end of the investigation. I took a deep breath, which came across very loud, being close to the recorder and, after that, a woman's laughter can be heard that sounded close. No one else was present except Sid and me, so who was it?

I turned on the ghost box.

I asked, "Anyone with us?"

Male voice: "Yes."

"What is your name?"

Male voice: "Bur—" Could this have been Burgess, the first mayor of Petersburg? I heard a distinct "Bur," but the rest was cut off, or maybe it was too softly said. I suspect it could have been him. Unfortunately, that doesn't make it definite without proof.

"Do you like those taking care of the place now?"

"Sure."

Except for the EMF meter light coming on, nothing else occurred in that room or the rest of the second floor.

Third-Floor Investigation

Looking up the stairs to the room where ghosts might be.

After checking out the third floor, we climbed the stairs that led to the room above the third floor. This is where runaway slaves may have been hidden, as it could have been an Underground Railroad spot.

I used the ghost box. "Give me your name?"

Female voice: "Sp–" (I couldn't get the rest, as the voice lowered.)

"Were you here during the Siege?"

Male voice: "Yes."

Female voice: "Yes."

"Were you caught during the Siege?"

Male voice: "No." Then the same man said, "Free."

When I felt freezing coldness against my back, I said, "I feel cold against my back. Is that you?"

Male voice: "Yes."

When the cold left my back, but appeared against my side, I asked, "Are you making my side cold?"

Female voice: "Yes."

"Are you the ones who scared those two boys taping downstairs when they spent one night here?" (Sid mentioned earlier that he'd allowed two investigators to stay one night so they could film and something has *whooshed* down the stairs to the third floor at them, scaring them to leave the building quickly.)

Male voice: "Yes, I did."

"Have you ever been downstairs to the shop and watched the people?"

Male and female voice together: "Yes."

I asked other questions after that and received no answers until I asked, "Why are you still hiding here? Why not head over... uhmm, what do they call the veil?" Of course, that was when the ghost box shut off. It appeared the spirits did not want to say anything else.

Rooms on the third floor.

Author Note

From Susan Schwartz, who critiqued my book: This may have been the place I was telling you about a couple of years back. I think there was an antique store in the bottom; I got a notion of being watched on the first floor, and asked the owners what was upstairs. They led me to this room that had a hole in the wall kind of thing and the owner told me they kept slaves in there and there should be activity. I didn't get anything from the slave wall, but there was a ghost following me or watching me up there in that particular room. I was pulled up there like a magnet. I think the owner thought I was a little off, but when I told him what I felt, he didn't seem surprised.

Hole in wall, where slaves using the Underground Railroad hid.

Want to have tea and scones like in England, but can't afford to go? Try the Blue Willow Tea Room in Petersburg—the tea is fine, the scones delicious with clotted cream, and the décor lovely. However, the place has more than just tea, it has spirits haunting its second and third floors, and they are way past the need for drinking tea.

VISITOR INFORMATION

Blue Willow Tea Room
104 West Old Street
Petersburg, VA 23803
804-733-7605
www.bluewillowtearoom.com

Hours of Operation: Wednesday thru Saturday 11 a.m. to 4:30 p.m.; Sunday 12 p.m. to 4:30 p.m.; Monday and Tuesday closed.

The Bistro at Market and Grove

ONE NEED NOT BE A CHAMBER TO BE HAUNTED.

—EMILY DICKINSON

The Olgers of Sutherland Tavern let me know that this restaurant had ghosts. They told me they found out after they'd dined in the building. The daughter, Emma, said something kept touching her leg and, if it had been an animal, it would have to find its way to where she sat. I called on the Fourth of July and made arrangements to come by on July 9, 2014, for an interview at 3 p.m.

The Bistro at Market and Grove Restaurant.

The Interview

I arrived at The Bistro at Market and Grove on that Wednesday in July to interview the owner and anyone else available who knew of the eerie happenings that concerned the building. I also wanted to perform a quick investigation to see what I would get. Since I arrived at 2:30 p.m., I had time to try their "special"—a

Reuben sandwich and a garden salad for an early dinner—while the owner, Russ Johnson, made a run to the bank. The food was superb. I took a few photos and caught a glowing oddity that actually had a reflection in the mirror behind it! I took another of the same spot, but got nothing in that one.

The glowing thing has a reflection in the mirror behind it!

I finished my dinner and Russ had returned. I joined him and my waiter, Fred Baker IV, and a worker from the kitchen, John Lucas, at a table by the window in the room with the bar to interview them about the hauntings.

Russ told me he assumed ownership of the restaurant in 2006. He remembered the building having a dark and foreboding feeling for the first year. A year later, after an exodus of employees, they began hearing laughter, felt chills, and, though the music is always turned off overnight, it would be playing the next morning when they returned. Many also felt they were not alone when they came to work early in the morning.

During the winter, the thermometer inside traveled up and down constantly for no reason. Customers would head to the bathroom and return to find the napkins they had spread across their laps gone. They searched under the table and elsewhere, but never found the cloths. This occurred for about a year, but this hasn't happened since the first couple years. Russ's keys would disappear and reappear a few times, but he thought that may be due more to him than any ghostly interference.

The dishwasher in the kitchen had been fixed so it could not turn off, unless you pushed the button. Russ's mother was washing dishes one time, when suddenly, the machine shot water at her face. It was impossible for the dishwasher to do this normally, and Russ tried to explain what happened to the repairman who came to fix the problem. The man called them liars.

A friend, Tammy, passed away. Six months later, they saw her one night out on the patio, smoking. She looked solid as any live person standing there in the dark, and then she just disappeared. Occasionally, some of the workers would smell the odor of marijuana, which Tammy liked to smoke. Russ also told me that a waitress, Lisa, had seen Tammy a couple of times, too.

A couple of groups of paranormal investigators had visited the restaurant before my investigation. One female ghost hunter snapped a photo in the dark dining room and got a female spirit in a long gown whirling around the room. Another time, some investigators agitated the female ghost to get her to respond, and a male ghost voice yelled, "Get out! Leave her alone!" When asked for his name, he gave the name Charles Holland. Shocked, Russ said that this was his great-uncle. There was no way the investigators could have known that, as he had not mentioned any family members to them.

One time, when they came in, they found an entire table setting on the floor smashed. Another waiter at the night investigation I conducted admitted that after putting a glass on a table, he'd watched it sail across a table and dive off, only to shatter on the floor.

The security system they employ at night has gone off a few times. Police would arrive to find what looked like someone running around inside. They'd called Russ who would drive to the place and unlock the door. No one would be seen; however, one morning when he entered the building he thought he saw someone darting out the back. He called the police who came and searched, but found no one. All of the cops left, except one, and he and Russ were in the dining room when they heard two women giggling. Funny thing: Russ and the policeman were the only people in the building!

Another time, Russ's nephew was dropped off close to midnight. The boy saw the woman in the long dress nicknamed Francine by Russ and his staff. She came up to him and touched his cheek. Russ said they all saw the see-through hand. Usually they only saw her face or flowing skirt.

After a server acted obnoxious, the glass tray behind him slammed into the back of his head—three separate times. He would push it back, continue to act nasty, and once again the tray punched the back of his head. Guess the ghosts did not like his attitude.

One day, Russ found what should have been a cold cup of coffee, only it was hot, as if just freshly brewed.

Afternoon Investigation
JULY 9, 2014

The interview done, I began an EVP session hoping I would get something concrete, but sadly, no voices. I thought that if I knocked and asked if they would knock back, they might do it. I heard some knocking, but assumed it could have been John Lucas, as he was working on something at the time.

I went into the ghost box session. Unfortunately, my tuning was off, and I tried to get it back to the right spot for scanning. When it was still off, I got static, and suddenly, a man's voice blurted out, "Satan." This response creeped me out.

Finally, I had the setting where it was supposed to be and started the scanning. I introduced myself, and had Russ, John, and Fred do the same. I'd hoped this would get the spirits to say their names.

I asked, "Who is here?"

This photo came out dark, even with the flash going off.

A woman answered, "Me."

"Was that Tammy?"

The same woman said, "Yes." Then the scanning shut off. Maybe she didn't want to talk further.

I reset the scanning and went on to ask if a man was with us. A man answered, "Yes." I asked if any other relatives or friends were there and received no response. I asked if Russ's great-uncle Charlie Holland was there. No one answered me.

I tried again. "Anyone else with us?"

Maybe the same man—he said, "Tammy."

I headed for the dining room to be alone and ask more questions. As I stepped into the dining room, a man yelled out from the box, "Pamela!" It was loud enough for me to hear audibly at that moment. I quickly remembered I had introduced myself earlier. At that moment, an odor reached me. I remembered what the one ghost liked to do, and tried to remember if marijuana smelled like that. Though I'd never smoked it, I had been at places back in the '70s where others did. I remembered a sickly sweet scent, and this one did not have that. It dissipated after a couple of minutes.

I stopped by a long table in the middle of the room. "Can you talk?"

A male voice: "You."

"You what? Are you asking me to talk further?"

Same male voice cussed. "Damn it."

I ignored the cussing. "Can you tell me your name, sir?"

Something was said, but it was too low for me to catch when I listened later.

I said, "Did I smell something when I came in here?"

The man replied, "Me."

"It wasn't Tammy smoking?"

Same man again answered, "It was me."

The elbow of my right arm grew very cold. I asked, "Is it you making my elbow cold? Are you standing close to me?"

The man said, "Tammy."

Then a male voice—I am not sure if it was the same guy or another—said "Philip."

I hadn't heard about any Philip in my interview with Russ and the others. (As I listened to all this on my recording, I planned to asked Russ when I returned to do a night investigation. Maybe the name might mean something to him.)

I asked, "How many female spirits are with me right now?"

The man said, "Two."

Just the mysterious woman in the floor-length dress and Tammy?
"How many spirits altogether?"
Nothing.
One last try, and that would be it for today. "Can you tell me your name?"
This time a woman said, "Tammy."
"Tammy, can you tell me your last name. So I can verify it?"
She wouldn't or couldn't give it.
"I am writing a book and wondered if you'd like to have me tell my readers anything, or is there something you would like known? What was important to you, what year you died, anything else..."
A voice that sounded faraway said, "I died."
I thanked the spirits and walked back to where Russ, Fred, and John sat. The men's restroom door was still open as it had been left. Russ and I agreed for me to return Saturday, July 12th, at night around 10 p.m.
I emailed some friends I had been on paranormal investigations with before and trusted. Three other people would be joining me.

My fellow investigators, Carol, Julia, and Leonard at the table we used in back of the dining room.

Night Investigation
JULY 12/13, 2014

I returned Saturday night around 9 p.m. and Julia Ogle and her boyfriend Leonard Price were already there waiting by their vehicle. The sky was clear with a few stars dotting it. About fifteen minute later, Carol Smith of Richmond Paranormal Society showed up. She had gotten lost, searching for the area. She was alone; her husband had remained home.

I convinced my three friends to accompany me to Peter Jones Trading Post, across the street from the restaurant. Since we still had about forty-five minutes before we could head into the restaurant, we would do a short investigation at the other spot. We ran into some Civil War soldiers there. (This investigation is the "Old Towne Petersburg's Other Haunted Places" chapter.)

We had arrived (gotten back to) at the parking lot, as I couldn't find my camera inside the pink bag I carried like a purse. Next, I tried the ghost bag, but it wasn't inside it, either. I opened my car and checked the front seats, but found nothing. I dug under the seats, the sides, and behind.

I called my husband Bill, thinking I must have left it home, even though I thought I had placed the camera beside my ghost bag on the passenger seat on the way to the investigation. Bill searched the house, but he could not find my camera. I grew frantic, so I took my flashlight and retraced my steps all the way back to the Peter Jones Trading Post where the Civil War spirits had told us to go, but I didn't find a sign of my camera.

One of the investigators, Leonard, searched my car from the passenger's side, and even underneath the vehicle. I asked the ghosts to bring back my camera, if they had taken it. I explained that I needed it and couldn't afford another at that time. When Leonard withdrew from the Corolla, I asked if he would take a look under Carol's vehicle. That was when I saw my camera in its bag for the first time, nestled against the back of his foot on the pavement. He felt it himself and gazed down, then picked it up to hand it over to me. I turned it on and was happy to discover nothing wrong with it. Both Leonard and I had stepped all around that area between my and Carol's vehicles and we'd never seen it—not until after I'd asked the spirits to bring it back to me. Had those phantoms at Peter Jones Trading Post done this, so we would not come back to take photos there? They had heard me say I had forgotten my camera and planned to return to my car to get it.

Leonard said, "That was creepy. We're not even at the restaurant yet, and already we've had a paranormal incident."

We crossed the street to The Bistro and entered. Inside the restaurant, we set up in the empty dining room. The only customers still there sat outside on the patio. After we got situated, I turned off all the lights, so the dining room would be dark as possible. I even drew the drapes to stop any outside light from entering the room. The strap of my Tigger™ watch broke when I switched off one lamp, and I pocketed it. The watch kept running all night when I checked it on occasion. (You will understand why I mention this when you come to the end of this chapter.)

The only light left came from the room we stepped into when we first entered the restaurant and the kitchen, but that door stayed shut, except when one of the workers walked in and out. I put one of my recorders in the men's restroom, where there has been some paranormal activity, and left it running.

My other recorder, along with the recorders of the others, were placed on the table along with our EMF meters. I sat down and invited Tammy to come sit with us and to light up a joint to put her at ease. We told her that we wouldn't mind if she did. I asked if anyone from the trading post ruins had followed us here. I inquired about the lady in the long dress, the one Russ and his workers called "Francine," who danced in the dining room. I asked if the dancing lady actually had danced at the Golden Ball Tavern across Market Street when this had been the warehouse of Peter Jones Trading Post.

I got up to shut off the fans, so we could see if that was what caused Julia's and my EMF meters' lights to have three lights on, not just the first one. We needed to take away the possible explanations before we thought about the impossible.

I switched on my ghost box and introduced my fellow ghost hunters, who sat around the dining table close to the fireplace and the free-standing air conditioner. I pointed at Carol sitting to my right. "Say hi to Carol."

A male voice came across my ghost box. "Hello."

I asked Julia to say hello.

Julia said, "Hi."

No one said anything back to her. I ask them to say hello to her, but still got nothing.

I asked if anyone was with us and told them to use my energy (I never ask spirits to use other people, unless they themselves give permission), if they needed help to do so.

I asked, "Is Charles Holland here?"

A woman's voice came across the box.

"Is that Tammy?" Nothing.

Then a man spoke across the box. "No." No, the woman I heard was not Tammy, but the other woman haunting the building?

"Who is this?"

The man spoke again. "Me."

"Is Tammy here?"

He said, "Yes."

"Do you know Russ? Who is Russ?"

The man replied, "The owner."

"Is this Charles Holland?"

"Black man."

Interesting. "Who is the black man?"

At that moment, Russ walked up to us.

I said, "Say hello to Russ."

The man said, "No."

"Why not? He's a nice guy."

The man said, "Sharp people."

All of us laughed.

Russ left us to return to the kitchen. I asked who was the woman that Russ and the workers called Francine. I asked her to give us her real name.

A woman's soft voice spoke over the box. "Ann."

Had we gotten the true name of the spirit who liked to dance in the dining room? "Are you the spirit who likes to dance in this very room? Did you come from the Golden Ball Tavern?"

"Yes." We never got anything else from her, at least not across my ghost box or Carol's. I am not too sure which spirit or spirits manipulated Carol's Ovilus we had on that night, either.

I sat more comfortably in my chair and asked, "Anyone with us have anything to do with Peter Jones Trading Post?"

A man said, "One."

"What is your name?"

"Peter." Peter? Peter Jones? Because the restaurant stood where his warehouse had been in the past. Did he still hang around?

I thought I heard a woman's voice through the box. "Is that Tammy or Ann?"

A man asked, "Why?"

I asked again. "Tammy or Ann?"

The man said, "Me."

"Who?"

"Phillip."

I chose another question to ask. "Who was the person who said, "Damn it" to me when I was here this past Wednesday? Was it Charles Holland by chance?"

What I got was "...out."

"Say each word slowly. Enunciate."

"Yes."

"Is this Holland?"

"Yes."

"Are you Mr. Holland?"

"You are...pretty," If truly Charles Holland, he hadn't cussed me out. I wondered who Phillip was. "Who is Phillip?"

"Phillip. Me."

I asked what his connection was. To us? To Peter Jones Trading Post? To one of the people to do with the restaurant? The man never did let us know.

I asked if Tammy wanted me to tell her friend, Russ, anything. A woman spoke. "Yes."

I asked her what she wanted me to tell him; however, a man's voice came on. I told him to let her talk. The word, "Woman..." came across the box. Woman? Me? Tammy? An insult? I countered with asking for Ann. Finally, frustrated, I asked, "How many male spirits are here?"

A woman's strong voice said, "Three!"

Not sure about Ann, but I suspected that had been Tammy, as being a modern woman, it would be her shouting that out. Later, Russ told us Tammy was not a shy person and wouldn't let anyone stop her from talking. I began to think the men seemed determined to speak a lot. With Russ standing there, I asked if Tammy would like to tell him something. A woman said, "Sure." The scanning shut off at that moment.

One of the guys?

I turned it back on and encouraged Tammy to talk to Russ.

Russ said, "Hey." A woman's voice came across the box, sounding far away, "Hello." He hadn't heard it at the time, but I did when I listened at home.

I asked how many female spirits were present? No one answered. I went on to tell Ann to dance and told the entities to use the box to speak. One male said, "Nope."

I prodded at the ghosts, telling them they could say any of our names. None of them did.

Suddenly a voice said, "Watch it."

"Watch the language or what?"

No one told us what that meant. Maybe, as another investigator pointed out, that ghost meant the other ghosts to watch their mouths.

I shut off the box completely and just kept my recorder going. I retrieved the other recorder and laid it next to the first one. Carol kept her Ovilus going. The waitress Keri joined us and she asked a question, "Am I safe?" The Ovilus said, "wicked, bishop, and foreign."

Russ told me something that might have to do with the first word I got off my ghost box from the investigation Wednesday. That word had been Satan. It seemed that whenever someone acted "slutty or bad," Tammy would say, "Satan." Strange how a word I've never heard from my box spouted in a place where one of its ghosts, while alive, always said that particular word—though it had come from a male phantom.

Going back to Carol's Ovilus, we didn't always see the connection to our investigation, though some of the words appeared to be related. Words like "appetite" appeared several times. The place we were investigating was a restaurant. Another time, in connection to the black man that came across my ghost box, her Ovilus said, "slave, head, slain." As Russ pointed out, not far away from the restaurant, a slave auction had existed. Also at the river side of the trading post, some slaves had been discovered in a man's ship. The man had been paid to help them escape north until he ran aground. Had some slave been hit over the head and killed near here? Leonard noticed the names Betty and Kate, and he asked Russ if either seemed familiar. Russ's eyes widened and he acknowledged that Betty was his mother's name. He didn't know the name of Kate. Earlier in the night, when Carol told Ann she could dance, the Ovilus came up with "After" and "Hunting." Carol wondered if that meant the spirit would dance, only after our investigation was over.

At one point during the investigation, I spotted my name roll across Carol's Ovilus. That had been the second time this week that I'd heard or saw my name in this place.

Carol switched on her ghost box and asked, "Would anybody like to speak to us on my ghost box?"

A voice said, "No."

Other words were said: "Hey there" and "Go." Carol ended up shutting off her box.

I tried to tempt Ann to join me by getting up to dance. My arms out, I twirled around the dining room. Getting no response, visually or audibly, I returned to my seat and picked up my camera. I switched its setting to film video.

Beginning to videotape, I aimed the camera toward the doorway between the dining room and the first room. At one point, blue lines flashed across the screen and I pointed them out to Carol, explaining I had gotten lines in still photos on occasion at haunted spots like that. Through the viewfinder, I watched as the waitress opened the door that led into the kitchen. At the time, I hadn't seen anything. But later, as I watched the video, I saw at first one, then another, shadowy figure speed quickly from left to right. Shocked and elated at the same time, I backed up the video to view it again. Russ was in the kitchen at the time that Keri was walking through the doorway into the kitchen, and Carol, Julia, and Leonard sat around the table. I think I had gotten two spirits running directly in front of me. Close, too. I could have reached out and touched them. After that passing, I saw myself bring the EMF meter into view with only two lights showing. The shadows had been in frame for maybe a second or two. Later, I showed the video to my son, Chris, and he said it looked like a hand passing in front and asked if any of the others had moved into the frame. I explained that none of us had done anything like that—the only time my hand passed in front of the camera was seconds later when I picked up the EMF meter to see if I could get more lights to show on it. Had there been two separate figures, or a single figure, then the second one a hand pressed close to my camera? Maybe Ann was doing her dance, then another spirit, or even her, trying to keep my camera from filming her.

Russ walked out of the kitchen, followed by Keri and while she waited for him in the other room, he came into the dining room to tell us he would be gone about fifteen minutes to take her home, as her husband was working late at his job and couldn't pick her up. He would lock the doors and lower the lights in the other room, as sometimes that helped bring out the ghosts.

Before he left, I snapped four photos of the patio outside, since all the customers had gone, and then let him lock the front door.

Once he drove away, I viewed the outside through the glass windows in the dining room and only saw a dark-filled empty world, lit only by streetlights. Inside the room with the bar and lowered lights, felt as though some invisible entities waited and watched us.

We kept our eyes on the doorway and, at one point, something flashed from my left to right by the strip of black mat in the other room. Julia saw it; however, Carol didn't. She said it must be a car that drove by seconds later, and the flash had been its lights. I said, "I saw the occurrence before the car had come by." Her Ovilus spat out "Blind" at that moment, which made her laugh.

I suggested that maybe it had been the see-through bottom of a woman's skirts we saw as she had scurried from one end of the room to another. Leonard and Julia investigated the other room, but they never found whatever it had been.

The Ovilus spouted "Lady." I asked if that had been Ann we had seen earlier. "Truth" came across the Ovilus.

Russ returned around 1:30 a.m., and the four of us turned on the dining room lights and gathered our equipment. Julia and Leonard left quickly, with Carol and me walking out the door, and Russ on our heels. We thanked him for having us and bade him goodbye.

After about fifteen minutes driving over the bridge into Colonial Heights and through the city to Chester, I made it home shortly after 2 a.m.

Full moon over building next door to The Bistro. See the mist over the edge of The Bistro's roof? It was a clear night that night. Paranormal?

An extra note: when I got up the next morning, I checked my Tigger watch for the time. The watch's battery had died at 1:30 a.m., the same time we had left the restaurant. Coincidence? Another interesting thing about that night was that it was the first night of the full moon. I had wondered if full moons helped paranormal activity develop and mentioned this on my Facebook page. Two people said yes.

Next time you eat at the restaurant, don't be surprised if a phantom joins you at your table. Even ghosts get hungry.

VISITOR INFORMATION

The Bistro at Market and Grove
422 N. Market Street (in Old Town Petersburg)
Petersburg, VA 23803
804-732-4480
www.facebook.com/pages/The-Bistro-at-Market-and-Grove/99642348471

Hours: Sunday 10 a.m. to 2 p.m.; Monday closed; Tuesday 11 a.m. to 9 p.m.; Wednesday 11 a.m. to 9 p.m.; Thursday 11 a.m. to 9 p.m.; Friday 11 a.m. to 10 p.m.; Saturday:11 a.m. to 10 p.m.

Dodson's Tavern

A TAVERN IS A PLACE WHERE MADNESS IS SOLD BY THE
BOTTLE.

— JONATHAN SWIFT

Dodson's Tavern.

Built in 1753 by John Dodson, the house at 311 High Street remained in his family until 1972. That was when Colonel John Cargill Peagram (who people believe stayed at the home for a short while) passed away at the age of ninety-one. There are those who say his ghost still haunts the building, making sure people are taking care of it. Could it be someone else? Could the building have more than one spirit? Burglar alarms go off for no reason, and books from the library are found scattered around the room, even though they were on the shelves earlier.

Now the word "tavern" is misleading. Dodson's was actually an "up-scale" boarding house similar to Williamsburg's Raleigh Tavern. *Tavern* was the term used in Southern regions for those in urban settings, while those in the country were called "ordinaries." It is one of the few Federal structures in the Petersburg area with an interior that has remained basically unchanged for more than 200 years.

The floors and stairways are believed to be original with the stairways boasting delicate Federal motifs and wrought-iron supports. Double doors are at the end of the hallway, and multi-paned window doors have recently been added where exterior shutters would have been. These changes all bring more light into the hallways.

The stair treads on the steps leading to the English basement are original, as are the basement windows, some of its panes, and a corner cupboard in the Tavern Room. A few baseboards have been replaced. The fireplace had been bricked up and was discovered when the house was renovated in the late 1970s. The rear of the house has the initial kitchen and slave quarters.

Among those who have stepped into the Tavern are Aaron Burr and his daughter Theodosia, who stopped there on their travels south, following Burr's famous duel with Alexander Hamilton. It is said that Theodosia made her famous cakes while staying here. Another person who stayed was noted watercolorist William Simpson, and he lived in the place with his family for eleven years. One of his paintings still hangs over the mantle in the dining room.

On January 21, 2011, I drove to Petersburg to take some photographs for this book. I snapped some pictures, and then stopped to stare at the tavern before climbing back into my car parked across the street. Nothing unseen stared out through any of the windows at me, nor did anyone—living or unliving—from the house or anywhere else on the street.

In 1994, it was reported that the owners of the house talked about things vanishing and then reappearing later. When a visitor to the house passed a mirror, they stopped in shock, as they saw a figure in garb from another era in the glass—and not them!

A granddaughter had visited the family and stayed the night. The next morning she asked her grandmother why she kept peeking in on her. But, of course, it wasn't her grandmother.

When one of the owners first moved to the place, she heard the front door open and close. From behind her, she heard three heavy footsteps and the thud of a duffle bag hitting the floor. She whipped around, but saw no one. It was later she learned from the neighbors about the house's haunted reputation.

It is said, back when the place was used for overnight guests, one traveler bragged about having a bag of gold; the next morning, he was found with a slit throat. A slave was accused of it and lynched in a tree behind the house. It is said that the slave's ghost haunts the grounds, maybe seeking revenge.

There are even stories that Captain Peagram, or Aaron Burr, or his daughter Theodosia could still be wandering the hallways. Maybe they are still happily haunting the tavern. Next time you're in Petersburg and happen to be walking past the building, glance at the house. If you see a curtain move at one of the windows, it most likely is one of the living residents, nothing more. Then again, maybe not!

VISITOR INFORMATION

Dodson's Tavern
311 High Street
Petersburg, VA 23803

The location is now a privately owned home and not open to the public

Trapezium House

THEIR WAY TO ME. 'TIS FALSELY SAID
THAT THERE WAS EVER INTERCOURSE
BETWEEN THE LIVING AND THE DEAD.
— WILLIAM WORDSWORTH

Trapezium House.

The Trapezium House is located at 15 West Bank Street in Petersburg and is like the Winchester House in California, but on a much smaller scale. It was built by Charles O'Hara in 1817. A few years ago, I ran into someone who told me that one Halloween they'd allowed people into the Trapezium House. She said when she went in, the ceiling was low and odd, and the place was crazy.

The legend concerning the house incorporated O'Hara's West Indian servant's beliefs that a trapezoid-shaped building would ward off ghosts and evil spirits. The workmen must have thought him loony when he had them build it.

Charles O'Hara left Ireland at the age of nineteen and immigrated to the West Indies, while amassing a large fortune. History does not record the reason

Charles O'Hara's Gravestone at Blandford Cemetery.

he came to Petersburg, or even how many West Indian servants came with him. It is known that he did bring a West Indian woman named Jinsie Snow. It is she who is believed to have told him to build the unusual house.

With no right angles and no parallel walls, the steps of the stairs that lead up to the upper floors are set at odd angles with the wall. There is supposedly only one room on the first floor and two rooms each on the other two floors. The interior is elongated, which could be an accident of the house's irregular shape or a deliberate plan. The windows, fireplace, and staircase are all off center. There is only one door in the front. The oddest feature is that the cellar, where the cooking had been done, could only be reached by a trapdoor under the stairwell. The ceiling is only four feet high, which must have made it difficult for anyone over that height to walk around.

O'Hara, dressed in full British uniform, would sit on the front porch on important English and Irish holidays. This is most peculiar as it is said that the man never served in the military, so why the uniform? Because of this, he became known as "the General."

He only lived on the first floor and never swept or cleaned the floor. The house earned the nickname, "Rat Castle"—not just because of the obvious mess, but because he also kept rats, along with parrots and monkeys.

When he died, some people (being nice) took up a collection to mark his grave because the state took his fortune and the house. A tombstone with a harp as a symbol of Ireland marks his grave at Blandford Cemetery on Cockade Avenue. I found his grave and the stone at Blandford on Monday, June 9, 2014. It lies at the corner of Cockade Avenue and Crater Road.

Next time you think you live in an odd house, drive to Petersburg, and get a gander of the Trapezium House. Like the Winchester House, it too was built with ghosts in mind.

VISITOR INFORMATION

The Trapezium House
15 West Bank Street
Petersburg, VA 23803

The House is privately owned and not open to the public.

Old Towne Petersburg's Other Haunted Places

NO. THE MENACE OF THE SUPERNATURAL IS THAT IT
ATTACKS WHERE MODERN MINDS ARE WEAKEST, WHERE WE
HAVE ABANDONED OUR PROTECTIVE ARMOR OF SUPERSTITION
AND HAVE NO SUBSTITUTE DEFENSE.

—SHIRLEY JACKSON

1 West Old Street

An antique business is located at 1 West Old Street. It has separate apartments upstairs, like many buildings in Old Towne Petersburg. But more than the living work and live there. The dead still hang around.

Larry King, who works at Antique Genius at 23 West Old Street, at one time lived in a loft above 1 West Old Street. He told me that weird stuff would happen—a lot—in his apartment. His dog went crazy many times, barking at things he never saw. Small items of furniture would vanish and King would find them elsewhere in the place. In the mornings, he awoke to find pillows from his couch on the floor. He stated that his dog didn't do this, as each night he would lock the pooch in another room. He moved out in 1998 and someone else lives there now, but he always wonders if that person is having the same experiences he did... He has never asked.

Whether due to the building, or maybe even the pieces they sell, being haunted is all a part of the antique business.

Antique Genius
23 West Old Street

One may think they can escape the paranormal if they move, but sometimes, they can't—as the owner of Antique Genius at 23 West Old Street learned when he moved a few doors down to get away from paranormal activity. He didn't get away from being haunted.

When the tour guide of the Petersburg Haunts Ghost Tour led us past an open doorway, he recognized the person there from another address back up the street. The man had moved his antique business to this new spot. Excited, the man fetched a photo he'd taken in the building and pointed at a face looking down from the ceiling.

Later, I stopped by to find out about any more experiences he'd had there. The owner wasn't in, but his worker was. I shot some photos of the place, but found nothing in them. I tried again and again to talk to the owner, but we always missed each other. Finally, I gave up.

Later, one early Monday afternoon in 2014, I walked past 23 West Old Street and I noticed that the antique business no longer occupied the building. A couple of men were bringing in clothing and other things for what would be a clothing retail establishment. I didn't stop to ask them if either of them had any unusual experiences and I'm not sure where the former owner went with his business—hopefully to a spot that had no ghosts. But then again, owning a business dealing in antiques just might mean they might have left with him.

Spirits can be attached to antiques because the phantom as a living person owned the antique. The antique can be any size: as big as a cupboard to something as small as a ring. An antique business is full of antiques. Makes one wonder how many ghosts really haunt this store.

Peter Jones Trading Station

I found the remains of what is quite possibly the oldest building in Petersburg: Peter Jones Trading Station is believed to have been built between 1650 and 1750 as the western-most trading post. This site continued to have importance

What is left of the Peter Jones Trading Post.

through the Civil War when it was used as a prison and hospital. It housed captured Native Indian Federal soldiers from Michigan and Confederate soldiers serving punishment for military offenses. After the war, it resumed trading activities.

The Appomattox River was a busy trade route, and boats continued to visit Petersburg as far north as the site of the trading post until the 1930s. The site served a variety of purposes, lastly as part of a granary gutted by a destructive fire in 1980. Most of the building was destroyed in that fire.

There is a painted mural on the building facing Old Street that is an artist's impression of the Petersburg waterfront on the Appomattox River, most likely at the city docks.

I first visited in the winter and later returned on a hot, humid afternoon on June 9, 2014—this time to do an EVP session. The area was free of people and I kept to the shade as much as I could, but it didn't stop the humidity from following me.

I asked a series of questions. "Is Major Peter Jones here?" "When did you die?" "Peter Jones?" No answer to any of them.

I wandered down to an area that looked like a cell. No one said a word. "Any of you still here? Can you leave me a message?"

Later at home, as I listened to my recording from that day, I heard this twice: "Are...still here. Are...still here."

It was not a male voice and it was not my voice. I don't know what voice it could have been. I heard that women sometimes joined the army of both sides to fight. Had a woman in uniform been brought there to be jailed and wanted to let me know she still hung around?

I asked a few more questions that did not receive responses. Sweating from the nasty humidity, and feeling hungry too, I struggled through the heat to my car.

The Investigation

The night of the investigation at The Bistro at Market and Grove on July 12, 2014, across the street, Carol Smith, Julia Ogle, Leonard Price, and I met in the parking lot. A full moon hovered in the sky above.

Since we weren't supposed to go into the Bistro restaurant until 10 p.m., we gathered our equipment and made our way over to Peter Jones Trading Post. Our recorders already on, I turned on my ghost box and began asking questions to see if any spirits still lingered. Carol and the other two used their flashlights to read the posted signs for tourists about the ruin's history.

I asked, "Is there any spirit still here?"

A male voice came across the scanning waves. "Jacob."

I said, "Is Peter Jones still here?"

Peter Jones did not reply, so I said, "Jacob? Can you talk to me?"

He answered, "Jacob." Two other, different male voices followed his. "Phillip." "Harry."

I pressed, "Peter? Is Peter here?"

Nothing from Peter Jones came across the box.

We wandered down the street, ending up by a stone bench with bars crossing the front. I dropped all but my ghost box on the bench.

"Jacob? Jacob, are you one of the Confederates or Federal soldiers held prisoner here during the Civil War?"

"Yes."

"Tell us anything you want us to tell us. Are you a Confederate soldier? A Union soldier?"

The box stopped scanning. Occasionally, I found spirits could turn off the ghost box, whether due to not wanting to talk to us or some other reason. Sometime, I wondered if they were maybe drawing the power from the batteries and electronics.

Julia asked: "Who was here during the War? Confederate? Federal?"

A man with a deeper voice than the others said, "Both."

"Was Jacob one of the Federals or a Confederate?"

"Yes." That did not answer my question, just that he was a soldier.

Then the same man's deep voice came across the box, saying, "You must..."

I questioned, "You must what? We must go?"

I heard the man say, "Yes."

I asked if we could take picture and then we would leave them alone. I searched in my pink bag for the camera in its soft case, but it was not inside. It had to be still in my car, so I told my friends that I was heading back to the parking lot to fetch it. Carol's equipment was still in her vehicle, so we all left the structure. (We had a freaky paranormal experience in the parking lot that you can read about in The Bistro at Market and Grove chapter.)

What is left of the building can be found at the corner of Old and Market Streets in what might be called a small park setting. It doesn't cost to visit and who knows, maybe the phantom of Peter Jones or some Civil War prisoners might talk to you. You never know.

Haunted High Street

High Street has more than Dodson's Tavern to make it haunted. There are stories of a Confederate soldier's ghost that has been seen by people walking past the 400 block of High Street. Is he still guarding his post? At another home in the block, a feminine phantom is said to throw curtains around a room and unhinge doors. Wonder if she is upset about something?

There are more supernatural occurrences spooking up other homes along the street. Owners of one place found their dog locked in a room upstairs, knowing they'd locked the canine in a room downstairs prior to their leaving. Even if the dog was one of those pets able to unlock doors (like you see on YouTube or television), the lock to the downstairs room could only be unlatched from the outside.

Another person discovered a heap of coins in a corner of a room of their home and figured out they were not left there by any earthy ways. He took the coins away, but the next day located more stacked in the same corner. Possibly the spirit felt they owed the owner for something? Maybe the coins are for a haunting rent?

The Baltimore Row Houses, near the intersection of Market and High Streets, have more fire and deaths than any other place in Petersburg. Residents claim that they hear doors slamming when there is no wind and no one around. Coins are found in the corners of rooms in other houses, too. Could this be the same entity mentioned earlier?

UFOs Over Petersburg

A cigar-shaped object was observed for ten minutes over Petersburg on January 20, 1955. Then, more recently; a strange, large black rectangle with pulsing green lights and possible time dilation was spotted November 11, 2011. On August 22, 2013, some people saw a ball of fire disappear in the night sky around ten p.m. over Petersburg.

Centre Hill Mansion

THE MORE ENLIGHTENED OUR HOUSES ARE, THE MORE
THEIR WALLS OOZE GHOSTS.

—ITALO CALVINO

Centre Hill Mansion at night, during the Ghost Watch 2014.

Some homes retain just one spirit; sometimes there may be more. Centre Hill Mansion in Petersburg is one that holds many.

Centre Hill Mansion was first built in 1823 by Robert Bolling IV. Robert Bolling, traveling from England, arrived in America in 1660. His first wife, Jane Rolfe, was a grand-daughter of Pocahontas and John Rolfe. They had one son, John Bolling II, beginning what would be called the "Red Bollings." John Bolling remarried Anne Stith who began the "White Bollings" line in 1861. Centre Hill Mansion descended down to members of the "White" line of the family.

Robert Bolling III and his second wife, Mary Marshall Tabb, settled down on a piece of land in the very heart of Petersburg. They built two frame houses on East Hill, side by side, though intentionally apart. Over time, Centre Hill Mansion was built in the middle. The Bollings called it "Bollingsbrook."

One of five children, Robert IV, married four times! His first wife was Mary Burton; his second, Catherine Stith, descended from John Stith. Sally Washington, who passed away one month after marriage, became number three. The last, Anna Dade Stith, happened to be the half-sister of his second wife.

Even with four wives, Robert IV only had five children. He joined the Virginia Militia at the age of nine during the Revolutionary War, was present at the surrender at Yorktown, served in the Virginia Legislature, and was on the Vestry of Bristol Parish for Blandford Church. He was 79 when he died in 1839.

Centre Hill passed to son Robert Buckner Bolling. Buckner had eleven children and served in the Virginia Legislature. He was a Vestry of Blandford Church and later, the Vestry of Christ Church. He was also a member of the Free Masons who met at Centre Hill. The remains of every Stith family member was laid to rest in the mausoleum he had built. The mausoleum included room for himself, Sara, his first wife, two other wives, and his oldest son.

The tunnel (that you can only see on the Ghost Watch tour) was put in by Buckner Bollings for bringing in supplies, instead of having to come in on the first floor where family and guests were staying. According to the family genealogist, Alexander Bolling, Buckner owned 500 slaves at the start of the War Between the States. It is believed he left before the siege began and lived at a retreat home in Fauquier County near Upperville.

With the fall of Petersburg, Centre Hill was occupied by Union troops, led by General George K.L. Hartsuff. President Abraham Lincoln visited the mansion on April 3, 1865. A meeting was held there eleven days before Lincoln's assassination to ascertain the local situation.

Buckner lived for sixteen more years after the end of the war. He passed away at the Staunton, Virginia, home of his second son, Stewart, having left Centre Hill to be managed by his third son, Townsend Bolling. The mansion was supposed to be sold and settled among the heirs, but some thought Townsend was not hurrying that along, so they brought suit against him and another brother, John. Eventually, the estate settled with all family getting their share, and Townsend received Centre Hill as his portion. Townsend never married and lived at the mansion until he passed away in 1893.

The family rented the house to Archibald Campbell Pryor and his family for ten years. From 1900 to 1901, Charles Hall Davis and his wife, Sallie Filed Bernard, rented it. They bought it from the Bollings in 1901.

It is Mrs. Pryor who spoke of the piano, or melodeon, that she heard, as if someone played many familiar tunes on it—but no one was near it. Another time, her son asked her at breakfast, "Mother, where is the pretty lady who came and sat on my bed last night?" He told his mother that the lady held his hand and talked to him. His description of her fit one of the female spirits seen at the window above the porch. They've never discovered her identity.

Davis was a lawyer, bank president, president of the Chamber of Commerce, secretary of Virginia Consolidated Milling Company, and land speculator. He and his wife remodeled many rooms in the mansion, as well as the staircase that is present today. Around 1910, he began to have financial problems with charges of mishandling funds at Virginia Consolidated Milling Company thrown at him. Though proven innocent, he also lost money through the takeover of a firm he'd invested in. He had to auction some of the furnishings at Centre to recoup his losses; however, not everything was sold. A pair of marble dogs was catalogued for the sale, but still guard the front porch of the house today.

As more problems arose, he sold off most of the surrounding lots that he'd subdivided in the 1920s and 1930, including homes around the place; however, this didn't help. In 1936, Centre Hill was sold at auction for $7,300 to Mr. W. J. Miller of Petersburg. Miller wanted to demolish the house, but public sentiment held his hand and he sold it to Mr. Edgar S. Bowling of New York. In turn, Bowling donated it to the Department of the Interior National Park Services to be used as a museum. He made the donation in his wife's name: Mrs. Joe McIlwaine Bowling. Later, in 1962, a nonprofit group took charge of it as Centre Hill Battlefield Museum. It was in 1972 when the City of Petersburg took it over with the understanding it stay a museum. Restoration began with much work done on it from 1974 to 1978 and, in 1978, it opened as a house museum. Sometimes it is much more. I was excited to learn that a scene from season one of the AMC television series *The Turn* was filmed at Centre Hill sometime after the 2014 Ghost Watch. I watched it off and on, and the tour guide never mentioned (or didn't know) what episode would be about Centre Hill, but that it would be within the first season beginning in April 2014. The second season begins April 2015. Season one is now available on DVD and is for sale on Amazon. With so much history behind it, no wonder the house is haunted. The ghost stories began when the Campbell Pryor family rented it. Though now, the museum's Ghost Watch is held every January 24, and the guides say soldiers from the 1812 War are marching into the house, upstairs, back downstairs, and out the door. There have had others identifying them to be Civil War soldiers, but it is hard to say. The paranormal activity surrounding these sightings are a form of atmospheric or residual haunting. Stuck in a loop in time, they appear to be on some mystical schedule and appear at the same time and place weekly, monthly, or yearly. Since the soldiers are heard, but never seen, no one will know of their marches unless someone gets a photo or actually sees them at their predestined marching time.

The first person to experience this paranormal marching activity was supposedly the Bolling family, but it was definitely the non-family owner, Davis, who held a party every year so his guests could listen for the footsteps at 7:30 p.m.

Another female ghost is seen at the window above the front porch. A site coordinator from 2006, Ann Brown, told me, "No one knows who she is and no one has ever found out."

I received newspaper clippings from Ann (she was the person who convinced Bill Martin to start a Ghost Watch in 1991). They didn't charge that first time or make reservations as they thought no one would come. That night, they were shocked to discover 700 people waiting. After that, they began to take reservations right after the first of January. The reservation list fills up fast, and prices seem to change from time to time. Check with Centre Hill in current prices for the Ghost Watch if you plan to participate.

Images have been captured and voices heard, both inside and outside the building, when no one was there. There was a photo taken of a visitor in the park across from the mansion: three streams of light arrowed down behind her, with the school in the background also lit up, even though no one was there, as this picture was taken at nighttime. In another photograph, arms are reaching out of the air at someone standing near a wall looking at a photograph. This walled area is also within the room where the museum displays pews from a church.

One time, back when the Pryors lived there, Mr. Pryor used a bedchamber for an office. He didn't get much sleep as invisible hands kept snatching the blankets and tossing them to the floor whenever the lights were turned off. Three pianos were located throughout the mansion, and one family reported hearing one of them being played when no one was around. They checked it out; however, they found nothing but silence.

A photographer from the *Progress Index* came to take pictures and when he tried to get shots on the second floor, his camera wouldn't work. When he went back outside the house, the camera worked fine.

An assistant for Laura Willoughby, the Curator of Collections back in early twentieth-first century, always poked fun about the ghosts, as she didn't believe in them. Two days before I came to the museum, in 2006, she had been upstairs in the front parlor. She turned around and saw a skirt scurrying away. Afterwards, she told Ann that she would never laugh about the ghosts again.

Another time, two ladies visiting the museum went in and found no one around, so they went upstairs to find the gift shop. They came back downstairs to find Ann, and they complained about the woman who wouldn't let them in. Ann said, "There is no one upstairs." Both ladies left, shocked. Another time, in 1995, a man restoring the fanlight for the upstairs window felt as if someone was staring at his back. Ann thought it might have been Bolling making sure he did the job right!

One visitor found water droplets on the banister and wiped at them, saying she thought them to be tear drops. She also told the newspaper she had seen a woman's face in the window and heard marching boots. Another woman from Colonial Heights admitted to feeling a presence on the stairwell when she attended a Ghost Watch. Sandi Bosha and her friends attended one Ghost Watch, after feeling a presence in the museum on a prior visit. A friend brought a compass and the needle would move in several areas of the house: one spot was near a crib in a bedroom on the second floor and also in one of the back bedrooms. Another friend admitted to feeling the presence of a woman with a child in the crib room. Her opinion was that the woman wouldn't leave the house, as she was searching for the child.

Over the years, doors have opened for no reason, people have felt a presence, and a woman would be seen looking out the window. A tour guide, Evelyn Franklin, told of the time a table lamp on the third floor began to sway back and forth, moving slowly at first, then going faster, the crystal prisms clinking into each other.

I took the Ghost Watch tour on January 24, 2008. Our tour guide took us through the house and the tunnel used by servants (never seen on normal tours during the year). On the second floor, I had an encounter with "something" in one of the rooms. I was completely alone. All of a sudden, the chandelier above went into a full-out fast and hard swing, back and forth. I smiled, shook my head, and said, "Okay, you're showing off for me." I walked out of the room through a second doorway. Was it the female spirit or someone else? Not having a recorder yet to catch EVPs or ask any questions, I will never know.

My husband and I attended the Centre Hill Ghost Watch the night of January 24, 2014. During this event, I brought along my recorder, hoping to get some EVPs. Most of it ended up sounding mechanical. I am not sure if it was due to the place itself, but I definitely think the sounds were not paranormal in nature. The only odd thing that I captured that evening was at the beginning of my recording when I heard an odd pounding, like something knocking on walls. I cannot prove what it was. Yes, there was a group of people, but no one knocked on walls or doors. Everything else heard on the recording was our footsteps, our tour guide Janet Perkins speaking, and the rest of us talking and whispering—along with many other noises that anyone could logically identify.

I think having a personal tour might get more results from the apparitions than the ghost tour. I felt something there, but not enough to manifest for us or my recorder—unless you count the knocking that I can't explain.

When my husband and I visited Centre Hill for its Christmas Open House on December 7, 2014, I learned from a docent that on the last tour of the Ghost Watch back in January of the same year, around 8:45 p.m., they had a paranormal incident. The last tour group for that night was still on the first floor and was being led by their guide from the room closest to the front door into the next room. Just then, the shutters on the first window in the room they had just vacated flew open. Everyone screamed, as they all saw it. No one was near the window when it happened and there was no way the shutters could have opened on their own.

Another docent admitted to me that one time when he was on the first floor, he heard footsteps coming from the second floor. Thinking someone was up there, maybe even another docent, he went upstairs to check to see who it was. He found no one up there.

I was already familiar with most of the ghost stories; however, I wasn't aware of the update that the ghostly soldiers might be from 1812 and not the Civil War. But honestly, there is no proof which era the ghost soldiers come from when they relive those marching moments. But if you have never been there, take the regular house tour, and then come back for the January 24th Ghost Watch.

Centre Hill Mansion is all about history, and its spirits are a part of that history. Don't be surprised when you visit if you see a woman in white staring out of the window above the porch. No, it's not one of the docents at the museum; it is a phantom giving you an ectoplasmic welcome.

VISITOR INFORMATION

Centre Hill Museum
1 Centre Hill Avenue
Petersburg, VA 23805
804-733-2401
www.petersburgva.gov/index.aspx?nid=394

Tours are offered every hour on the hour. Last tour at 3 p.m. Check for updated price changes for activities.

Not Every Historical Place Is Haunted!

HAVE I PERSONALLY SEEN A GHOST? NOT A ONE.
—DAN AYKROYD

The house—taken on June 9, 2014. A real fixer-upper.

Not every building has paranormal activity, even if it is a historical place. That is exactly what paranormal investigator Jackie Tomlin and her team, Central Virginia Paranormal Investigations (CVAPI), discovered for themselves.

A local realtor called them, in 2009, to investigate a historical house in Petersburg to determine if it was haunted. It was a new listing and haunted houses appeared to sell well. There seemed to be no reports of anything supernatural attached to the building, but the realtor and the owner wanted to be sure. The place sat on a block rich in history, and it had been abandoned for a long time.

It needed heavy renovation, except for the entrance that contained the original three-story, beautiful stairwell that appeared structurally sound. Almost every room had broken windowpanes. There were weak or soft spots in some of the floors making it hard to walk. The team could see some of the original plaster beginning to fall and a lot of debris—glass, dust, and plaster—covered the floors. They could also see signs that the homeless used the building, too. It would not be a safe place to investigate.

CVAPI didn't know the media had been told of this investigation and they arrived to many spectators. This made audio review recording very time consuming, and with the light mist on the night air, the house certainly gave the impression of being properly haunted.

CVAPI consisted of not only believers, but skeptics as well, who all entered each investigation objectively. This one was no different. They came to gather evidence to review, not prove if it held paranormal activity or to disprove. Besides using their own equipment, they interviewed the neighbors, who reported never having seen nor heard anything out of the ordinary relating to the house or their own homes. The audio the group recorded was nine hours long, and the video, twelve hours. They had no electric power, but were able to run nine surveillance cameras from Jackie's truck. Members carried three walk-around cameras. Numerous still-frame cameras were used as well. Evidence the investigator group gathered, they found they could explain away via cool drafts in one of the rooms on the main floor that, at first, they thought was paranormal, but wasn't; they figured out that the basement that was full of water was the cause of the power loss. Within the three stories and basement, the only spike they got with an EMF meter concerned a spot in the kitchen. Further investigation found the wall backed up to the main power breaker and, though shut off, the power line still produced EMF spikes. Screaming on audio was noted by two of the investigators, but it turned out to come from the street at the time of the occurrence. In front of the monitor, someone reported that one of the cameras had moved on its own, but later review showed from another camera's viewpoint that someone had gotten their foot tangled up in the camera cord.

It is not normal for CVAPI to come out of an investigation without EVPs, but this location had none. This group does not consider orbs a sign of the paranormal; however, they do look for certain patterns on the video footage, but the video yielded nothing and showed no direct orb activity. A tremendous amount of dust due to falling plaster was evident.

Even the still photographs generated nothing in the way of evidence that could not be explained. Four images held promise and were sent away to professional photographers; however, they came back with logical reasons for their appearances.

This house in Petersburg proved to be nothing more than a creepy-looking house without a ghost. It's always best to keep a clear head when hunting for spirits—lest there be none!

RESEARCH INFORMATION

You can learn more about Central Virginia Paranormal Investigations and other investigations at www.CVAPI.com.

The Tombstone House

WITHIN, WALLS CONTINUED UPRIGHT, BRICKS MET NEATLY,
FLOORS WERE FIRM, AND DOORS WERE SENSIBLY SHUT;
SILENCE LAY STEADILY AGAINST THE WOOD AND STONE
OF HILL HOUSE, AND WHATEVER WALKED THERE, WALKED
ALONE.

—SHIRLEY JACKSON

The Tombstone House.

In Petersburg, there is another odd house besides the Trapezium House. The
Tombstone House was built in the 1930s, and is made of tombstones from
Poplar Grove National Cemetery. Located off I-85 at 1736 Youngs Road in

Petersburg, this house's exterior walls are fashioned from 2,000 marble tombstones of Union soldiers killed during the Siege of Petersburg.

I first found the house when I was writing *Haunted Virginia: Legends, Myths and True Tales*. The house was going to be in my last chapter on true stories that sound like myths and legends, but aren't. After all, who would believe that some builder would construct a house out of gravestones? My son, Chris, accompanied me that first time and remarked that the blocks looked like bricks to him; however, they are not.

To save money, the city sold these tombstones to builder O. E. Young for $45. The ones used to build the house were placed facing inwards, and then Young plastered over the inscriptions. He even made the walkway out of the tombstones that face down.

Wooden markers were placed upon the graves at Poplar Grove at first. Since wood is not a very durable material, the weather destroyed them over a couple of years. In 1873, the government replaced them with marble ones. The soldiers' names, states, and ranks were inscribed upon these new markers. Poplar Grove is the only cemetery in a national park where the tombstones lie flat.

While I was at Blandford Church doing the tour in 2010 for *Haunted Richmond II*, I learned from a docent that the house was haunted. The story she knew concerned a nephew of one of the owners. He had gotten drunk one night. His uncle told him not to drive home in his condition, but to sleep it off upstairs in one of the bedrooms.

However, when he awoke, he heard, "Charge!" He bolted up in bed and, to his shock, he saw a man dressed in a Civil War officer's uniform standing there. Seconds later, the man dissipated. He ran downstairs to tell his uncle about his experience.

The uncle shrugged and said, "That happens all the time."

Apparently, the spirits of the Civil War soldiers didn't want their tombstones taken from their graves. Or maybe their gravestones made up as a house is a more comfy place to haunt. This just goes to show that buying old gravestones to build a house isn't a wise choice. More than the living may inhabit the place!

This is a private home.

Battersea

Battersea Plantation House.

Battersea was the home of Colonel John Banister, the first mayor of Petersburg and a signer of the Articles of Confederation. Not much has changed since the late 1700s, the villa retains its original, elaborate Chinese lattice stair. The house is considered to be the finest example in Virginia. There is also a rare and significant one-story brick structure on its thirty-plus-acre grounds. Often mistaken for a garage, this is possibly the oldest standing orangery in Virginia.

It is believed that Reverend John Banister (1650-1692) was the original owner of the property. He was a clergyman and noted botanist, who had an

MA from Oxford. Sent by Henry Compton, bishop of London, he was to perform clerical duties in the New World in 1677. While having limited personal wealth, his scientific studies retained the sponsorship of wealthy and influential individuals, such as William Byrd I. Thanks to social and financial contacts, Reverend Banister and the Banister family become gentry of the area. The property he owned later developed into the Battersea estate.

After the reverend passed away, his son, John Banister II, was raised by the Byrds of Westover. He became a prominent planter and business associate of William Byrd II. Banister became a magistrate for Prince George County and vestryman for Bristol Parish in the 1730s. Banister was one of the original trustees of Petersburg.

After Banister returned to Virginia, he began a long career as a mill owner, as well as having a career in public service. He created an industrial complex of flour and saw mills on the south bank of the Appomattox River, just west of Petersburg, known as the Banister Mills. Ideally situated at the falls of the Appomattox River, the mills were quite profitable. They were already operating by the 1770s, because in 1775, Banister converted his saw mill for gunpowder production for the war effort. In the same complex, Banister operated a bakery and a coopering operation. Banister owned many slaves and probably employed craftsmen, such as coopers and millers.

As Banister prospered, he gradually assumed greater political roles. After serving as sheriff of Dinwiddie County, he became a justice of the peace for Dinwiddie in 1769. In 1764, he was elected to the vestry at Blandford Church and, in 1771, he was made a warden. Banister served in the House of Burgesses for Dinwiddie County with one brief interruption from 1766 until the Revolution.

Banister built a large and fashionable residence at his estate of Battersea in 1768, west of the town of Petersburg. At this time, Battersea was still in Dinwiddie County. The name "Battersea" may have been derived from an estate in England by the same name, which introduced and sold many plants and vegetables to Virginia. This would have been fitting considering the horticultural interests of Rev. John Banister, the first owner. Battersea was considered the "most handsome" house in the Petersburg area prior to the Revolution. In addition to Battersea, Banister owned Hatcher's Run, which he had inherited from his father and which was located in Dinwiddie County, a few miles southwest of Petersburg. Banister also owned a plantation in Prince George County called Whitehall, several lots in Petersburg, and land in Kentucky. Following the death of his second wife, Elizabeth Bland Banister, John married Ann "Nancy" Blair of Williamsburg in February 1779. They had two sons, Theodorick and John Monroe.

Battersea was occupied by Major General William Phillips (the same man whose grave in Blandford has not been found) and his British troops after winning the battle. Each year in April, the city marks the anniversary with a Revolutionary War reenactment at Historic Battersea.

Even with financial losses during the Revolution, Banister emerged afterwards as one of Petersburg's wealthiest citizens. He held public office from 1782 until he resigned in November. Then in 1784, he served as the first mayor of Petersburg under its new charter. Petersburg's western boundary extended just far enough into Dinwiddie County to include the house at Battersea. The part of the Battersea estate west of the city line remained part of Dinwiddie County. During this time period, a massive two-level portico was built on the front of the house. It covered most of the center block.

Banister died of an unknown illness at Hatcher's Run September 30, 1788. He was buried there, too. Survived by six children at the time of his death—this included an eldest son named John, and John Monroe, from his prior marriage. His wife Ann left Petersburg. Elder son John did not act on the purchase option on Battersea provided in his father's will. The estate was not completely settled until 1828. John F. May, who owned the house then, cleared up the last details with John Monroe and Theodorick.

A Visit

On April 20, 2014, Bill and I drove to the 233rd Annual Revolutionary War Reenactment of the 1781 Battle of Petersburg held at Battersea. Every year on the third weekend in April, Battersea is the setting of a commemorative reenactment of the battle fought on April 25, 1781. Though it had been going on since ten in the morning, we arrived around 12:30 p.m., so we would be on time to see the battle reenactment that would take place at 1:30 p.m.

After I took a photograph of fellow visitor Charlotte Clarke and her mother at the foot of the staircase in the front entrance hallway, we talked. They'd been coming to the event to reenact at Battersea for some time and, in 2013, Charlotte had taken pictures of the inside of the house. I asked her if she had ever had seen anything paranormal there. She excitedly replied that she had gotten a few anomalies in some of the photos—like orbs.

After they left the house, I shot a few more pictures, then stepped outside on the back porch and down the cement steps to the backyard. I wandered around, snapping more photos—one of the pet cemetery (had three tombstones) and the buildings—and headed back inside the house by the side porch of the house that faced the building where people were grilling and selling food for the event. Alone in the house, though I did not have my recorder or ghost box with me, I still asked if any spirits lingered there, to let me know by sounds or other ways, by using my energy. I began to feel cold in the large room with the open doorway that led out onto the back porch, but not from a breeze, as the day was calm and warm. Flickering colorful lines flashed across my viewscreen as I shot several pictures. But when I went outdoors onto the back porch, they vanished. Was it due to the paranormal? I couldn't say, as it could be something explainable.

VISITOR INFORMATION

Battersea Foundation
29 W. Bank Street
Petersburg, VA 23803
804-732-9882
www.batterseafound.org

The historic house itself is located at the physical address of 1289 Upper Appomattox Lane, Petersburg, VA 23803.

Petersburg National Civil War Battlefield—Eastern Front

IT IS WELL THAT WAR IS SO TERRIBLE, ELSE WE SHOULD GROW TOO FOND OF IT.

—GENERAL LEE TO GENERAL LONGSTREET

Eastern Front Visitors Center.

The Department of Interior established Petersburg National Military Park in 1926. It continues to be a major tourist attraction and a vital component of the city's economy.

Petersburg was heavily involved in the War Between the States. The city was part of a siege for nine-and-one-half months with two battlefields connected to it: the Eastern Front and the Five Forks unit.

Those who died on the battlefields around Petersburg, were left where they were originally buried until after the Civil War. From 1866-1869, most of the Union dead were buried at Poplar Grove National Cemetery, and thousands of Confederate dead at the historic Blandford Cemetery.

The Richmond area has many battlefields, and Petersburg is no exception. Located south of Richmond, Petersburg was an important supply center to the Confederate capital, as it held five railroad lines and key roads. Both commanding generals, Ulysses S. Grant and Robert E. Lee, knew that if these were cut, Petersburg could no longer supply Richmond with much needed supplies.

During the time between June 15 to 18 in 1864, Grant and his Northern Army attacked Petersburg. It might have fallen if not for the Federal commanders failing to press their advantage and the defense by the few Confederates holding the lines. Lee arrived on June 18 and, after four days of combat with no success, Grant began siege operations. It ended up being one of the longest sieges in American warfare. The Union attacked both Petersburg and Richmond, straining the Confederate forces. Grant's army circled Petersburg and cut off Lee's supply lines from the south. The Confederates hoped that by hanging on to their position, the Union Army would tire sooner or later.

By October 1864, Grant had cut off the Weldon Railroad and continued west to tighten the noose around Petersburg. The approach of winter brought a general halt to activities, though there was the everyday skirmishing, sniper fire, and mortar shelling. Lee had only 45,000 soldiers to oppose Grant's force of 110,000 men in early February 1865. Grant extended his lines southwesterly to Hatcher's Run and forced Lee to lengthen his own thinly stretched defenses.

By mid-March, it became apparent that Grant's superior force would either get around the Confederate right flank or pierce the line somewhere along its thirty-seven-mile length. At one point, Southern commanders hoped to break the Union stranglehold on Petersburg by springing a surprise attack on Grant. This only resulted in the Confederate loss at Fort Stedman and would be Lee's last offensive of the war.

On April 2 of the following year, Grant ordered an all-out assault. Lee's right flank crumbled during the night. The final surrender at Appomattox Court House was only a week away.

Ghost Box Session

Unlike last time, when I went alone to the park for research on *Haunted Richmond II*, Bill joined me on March 2, 2014. It was a nice day—sunny and spring-like. We stopped at the visitor's center to pay the $5 car fee and get a map. I also purchased a couple of books—one on black Confederate soldiers—from their gift shop. While Bill watched the film they showed in the visitor's center, I grabbed some of my equipment and wandered behind the building to investigate the first area where many battles had been fought.

I went immediately into a ghost box session after a couple of people left the earthworks and headed to the parking lot, leaving the area empty. "Is there anybody here?"

A man's voice came across the ghost box: "Jeff."

"You said Jeff?"

"Jeff here."

"Are you Northern or Southern?"

"North."

"Did you die in a battle here?"

"Yes."

"Who else is with you, Jeff?"

"Pete."

"What is the number of your battalion?"

"14."

"Did I hear 14?" No answer.

I pressed on. "Jeff, what state are you from?"

"State?"

"Yes, state." Nothing, just static.

"When did you die?"

"3—2—" Static after that.

I couldn't be sure if that meant March 2 or something else.

"Can you tell me your last name, Jeff?"

"Yep." Then I heard something like *snake* or *slade*, but it was too low and had static.

"Did you have a wife or a girlfriend you left behind?"

"Yep."

"Her name?"

"Barbara."

I walked. "Any Confederates here?"

A man spoke. "Yes. Me."

"What is your name?"

"Doyle."

"Anyone else here like to tell me their name?"

"Pete, Jim...."

"Did you play cards with your comrades?"

One man said, "Yes." Another replied, "No."

"What food did you like to eat when you were alive? How about johnnycakes? Did you eat johnnycakes?"

"Eat. Johnnycakes? Yes, I did."

"Were you proud to serve your unit and to serve your part in the war?"

"Leave it..." I wondered what the man meant.

The sound of a train filled the air as I stepped off the wooden steps. "That's a train," I said.

A male voice came over the ghost box: "Yes."

The voices from my ghost box seemed to indicate that armies from both sides still fought, even though the Civil War had been over for more than 150 years—although maybe now, they no longer fought, but hung around together to watch the living visit the battlefield!

After stopping at the spot where colored troops had fought the Confederates (there was no EVP activity here), we drove to the next stop on the driving tour of the battlefield: Battery 9. I located a spot to be alone and turned on my ghost box.

"Anybody of the spirit world here? Can you give me your name?"

I got a deep male voice: "Patterson."

I asked for the year he died, if anyone else was there, and if he was part of the colored troops. Then I asked if he had fought in the War Between the States.

Same deep voice. "Yes."

Nothing else after that. I stepped inside the first shack, and I shut the door behind me. Switching off the ghost box, I left the recorder running.

I asked, "Can you give me a sign you're here?"

Two bumps were heard that sounded like someone knocking on wood. I never hear them live, so was this their way of letting me know they were with me?

I turned on the ghost box again and tried another session inside. "Any colored troops die here?"

"—done it." Not sure what that meant.

"Use my energy to help you manifest better."

"No."

"Who did you leave behind when you went to war?"

"Martha."

"Are you sorry you went to war?"

Two voices chimed in. One said, "Yes." Another replied, "No."

"How old are you? I am in my fifties."

"18."

Tears welled up in my eyes at hearing this one soldier's young age.

The Crater

We stopped at other places, but with only so much time to do it, I saved the ghost box and recorder for the last stop: the crater.

Arriving where the Battle of the Crater happened, we got out of the car. It looked very peaceful, not a place where terrible explosions occurred, along with a battle filled with tragic deaths.

The Federals exploded a mine in Burnside's IX Corps sector beneath Pegram's Salient on July 30, 1864. The mine blew a gap in the Confederate defenses of Petersburg, killing 361 Confederates and leaving a hole in the ground 170 feet long, thirty feet deep, and eighty feet wide. Everything started deteriorating rapidly for the Union attackers. Unit after unit charged into and around the crater. The Confederates recovered and launched several counterattacks led by Major General William Mahone. The break was sealed off. The Federals ended with severe casualties, and Ferrarro's division of black soldiers was badly mauled. Sadly, this had both sides battling for eight months of the siege. By the end of the siege, it was estimated 3,800 Union troops were reported killed, wounded, or missing, with 1,612 Confederate casualties. Major General Ambrose E. Burnside was relieved of command for his role in the debacle.

One hundred and fifty years later, the crater is nothing more than a shallow, grass-covered depression in the earth. But history doesn't lie about what took place here. It was a major battle that left many soldiers dead or maimed for life.

I turned on the ghost box. "Anybody here? Anyone from the spirit world? Civil War soldiers? Union? Confederates? Yes or no? Can you tell me?"

Finally, after all that, a male voice spoke: "Yep."

"What was the number of your company?

"Did you die in the explosion?"

"Yes."

"Did I hear a yes?"

"Yes."

I asked a few more questions, but if I got answers, static made it impossible to hear them. After I took some more photographs, we left the battlefield to head home.

At the 150th Anniversary of the Battle of the Crater—August 2, 2014.

Later, when my husband and I returned to the battlefield for the last day (August 2, 2014) of the 150th anniversary of the Battle of the Crater reenactment, one of the reenactors there told me that when he reenacted for the same event with his group in 2013, camping overnight, he awoke to gunfire early on the morning of the event. Funny thing, none of the reenactors were doing any shooting.

Reenactors at the 150th Anniversary of the Battle of the Crater.

Were the Confederates and the Union soldiers battling as they had done back in July 1864? I know for me, they were silent while I was there. Maybe they were watching the reenactors playing at what they earnestly did for real.

Bigfoot!

Not ghost related, but this story had more to do with Bigfoot. It happened in 1979. A young boy and his friends rode bicycles in the woods by Petersburg Battlefield Park. This was close to Fort Lee. The kids built a fort/clubhouse in what might have been an occupied Bigfoot nest, but they did not know it at the time. Several weeks later, one afternoon they were scared off by powerful shrieks and screams. Had the creature left the area as it grew more residential, then gone wild? It may be interesting to note that no one has complained of any large, hairy creatures around the battlefield nowadays.

The next time you take a tour of the Petersburg Civil War Battlefield—the Eastern Front—make sure to take in the history and nature. Enjoy a picnic at

Battery 9, the crater, or even Fort Stedman. Don't be surprised, though, if a Civil War soldier joins you and you think he's a reenactor—until you realize you can see through him. After going through a war subsisting on johnnycakes, salt pork, burned beans, and bad coffee, your picnic lunch might look pretty scrumptious to the dead.

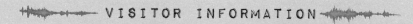 V I S I T O R I N F O R M A T I O N

Petersburg National Military Park
5001 Siege Road
Petersburg, VA 23803
804-732-3531 ext. 200

For GPS users enter 37 14' 37.87" N, 77 21' 24.87" W.

Blandford Church and Cemetery

LET'S TALK OF GRAVES, OF WORMS, AND EPITAPHS;
MAKE DUST OUR PAPER AND WITH RAINY EYES
WRITE SORROW ON THE BOSOM OF THE EARTH.
LET'S CHOOSE EXECUTORS AND TALK OF WILLS.
　　　　　　　　　　　　　—WILLIAM SHAKESPEARE

Blandford Church.

Blandford Cemetery and the Blandford Church has more than historic significance and fields of graves. It has ghosts. There is one legend about a man buried in a glass-topped coffin with his gravelot left unfilled. His mourning widow was able to visit and look upon him...except...one day, she met someone else and remarried. She replaced the glass top with a thick marble slab. Legend states that the slab never remained in place. Obviously, the man's spirit was upset about his wife's betrayal.

Of course, those who work there say they never saw this happen. Maybe his tale is nothing more than a made-up account that turned into a myth. Still, there has been ghostly activity.

When at this location before, while taking a tour for my last book, the tour guide paused in the cemetery to point out certain graves. One tombstone had lost a portion of its stone where a cannonball had struck it. Another was a mason's grave and had a symbol taken out of the gravestone. We learned of and saw the lovely harpist statue that marked the top of yet another grave. Were these dead rested, or were they restless? And yes, the guide that time did lead us to the site where the glass-topped tomb was laid—though it had no glass top—just a slab. Nothing spooky happened.

John!

When we stepped inside the church, our guide told us of her first tour and the paranormal incident that happened to her at that time. The only interment inside the church was that of Theophilus Field, one of the founders and a member of its vestry for over forty years. He was buried in the chancel of the church. She said the name, "John," and at that moment, someone pounded at the closed door right by her and the group.

"Go around to the front of the church to come in!" she called out, as she thought someone had been merely late for the tour.

No one answered or came through the front door to join the tour group.

When she said the name John again, another sound happened. That frightened her and she left the group, heading over to stand by the opened front door.

One of the tour members asked, "Is the church haunted?"

She just told them, "Come out of there."

The group didn't leave though. Still scared, the guide hollered from where she stood for the rest of the tour.

She admitted that she would never take another tour group into the church. But, one day, she was told she had to give a church tour, so she forced herself to take the chance. That was when the door knobs fell off the doors and she found herself locked in the place. She and Mr. Fields made peace that day.

Now since his name was not John, but Theophilus, I wondered why he took offense from her saying "John." Or maybe he thought she meant Theophilus and he was trying to correct her. We will never know.

I managed to take a couple of pictures and in one of them, there was an orb, plus the photo came out weird. It was blurry, even though I kept still when taking it. An old high school friend of mine met me at Martin's at Chesterfield Meadows and he told me that someone he knew had gotten married at Blandford Church. The person was told that they wouldn't be able to take pictures inside.

I thought it must be due to the stained-glass windows, but no, they were told that the pictures wouldn't come out. This did happen to people—all the pictures taken had come out blurry, when they shouldn't have...not unlike mine.

Some History

Blandford Church was established in 1735 as a seat of worship for Bristol Parish. Built of red colonial brick in Flemish bone, with glazed headers, the older generation clung to the notion that the brick had been brought over from England as ballast for sailing vessels.

Reverend Gorge Robertson was the first rector of Bristol Parish. His ministry was long: from 1720 to his death in 1740. His predecessor was Reverend John Banister. Banister owned land in the area and was a renowned botanist.

The church was built according to English ecclesiastical law, with the entrance door in the west and the altar in the east. The gallery over the door had been built for the slaves. Four pews in the north wing were for families of prominent church members.

The church building was abandoned in 1806, when membership in its congregation dwindled as a result of the consecration of a new church building in downtown Petersburg, where now the new courthouse stands. In 1882, due to the urging of Mr. William F. Spotswood, president of the city council, repairs were made to preserve the church, such as a slate roof replacing the original shingle one.

The city delegated the Ladies Memorial Association of Petersburg in 1901 to convert the old church into a mortuary chapel and a Confederate Memorial. This association was organized May 6, 1866. The first thing they did was to find a plot of land in which to bury Confederate soldiers. They secured the property in the eastern section of Blandford Cemetery as a gift from the city. Curbed sections for the different Confederate states, there were paved walks interspersed with circles and triangles for flowers and shrubs that the Ladies Memorial Association placed; granite markers denoted each state. Some of the markers were labeled "unknown." A granite arch was also set at the entrance to Memorial Hill.

Those who died at Fort Stedman on March 25, 1865, became the first burials on a plot just north of the brick wall surrounding the original colonial graveyard. The first Memorial Day was held June 9, 1866. Later, once Memorial Hill filled with the remains of the soldiers, on June 9, the whole section would be decorated with crosses, flags, and red and white flowers. Markers for the sections for those interred were marked "Confederates Soldiers 1861–1865." When all is said and done, 30,000 Confederate soldiers were buried on Memorial Hill inside the burial ground.

Mrs. John A. Logan, wife of General John Logan, saw this first Memorial Day in 1866 and, following her visit to Petersburg, she told her husband about it. It became his inspiration for the National Memorial Day that is celebrated the last Monday of each May (at that time May 30).

As part of the project, the association solicited funds from each former Confederate state for the creation and installation of a stained-glass window in the church in memory of the Confederate soldiers from that state. They secured the services of the famed Louis Comfort Tiffany, stained-glass artist, to design the fifteen memorial compass windows. He gave them a low price for the windows: $800 for the large ones, and $300 for the smaller ones. A representative was sent to check out the church and a decision was made to move the gallery over the north door. There would be fourteen windows, one to represent each of the thirteen Confederate states and one for Maryland, as it had been Southern in its sympathies. The fifteenth window was placed over the main entrance in the west, a memorial to the organization that developed this shrine showing the association's name and the date of the Civil War, a Confederate flag, and the year the association was formed, 1866, to the year the window was installed, 1909. Tiffany planned to have the state seal at the top of the window, along with the figure of one of the Lord's disciples in the body, and the state would prepare its own inscription at the bottom.

Each state was allowed to put in its own window, and all but Kentucky accepted. So Tiffany had a lovely cross of jewels installed in the last window, hung over the west door. It bears the inscription: "Glory to God in the highest, and on earth, peace, good will to men." It became known as the Tiffany "Cross of Jewels." As the sun sinks behind this window, the colors change with the glowing sun.

The first unveiled were the Virginia, Missouri, and Louisiana windows. This happened in 1904. The subject and theme of each window was left entirely up to the Tiffany studios. Each of the large windows contained the image of a Saint and symbols associated with the Saint, with the four smaller windows complementing the larger ones.

There are five other Confederate memorials in the form of plagues on the walls. A bronze plague to the right of the western entrance stated the gallery is a restoration done in memory of General Robert Edward Lee. Lee had sent a check to the association to aid them in their work in preserving and protecting the graves of the Confederate dead.

The cemetery's oldest marked grave dates from 1702. Among those buried within it is one foreigner: Major General William Phillips, British citizen and commander of the British troops during the April 25, 1781 "Battle of Petersburg." Phillips died on May 13, 1781, in Petersburg, due to a fever that might have been malaria or typhus. There's a memorial stone, erected by the Daughters of the American Revolution in 1914 that stands adjacent to Blandford Church. It marks the general location of Phillips' secret burial, done at the direction of his deputy commander, Brigadier General Benedict Arnold. The McRae Monument was erected in 1856 by the citizens of Petersburg over the burial site of Captain Richard McRae. This honored him and the Petersburg Volunteers for their efforts in the War of 1812 in Canada, especially in the battle of Fort Meigs. This is why to this day, Petersburg is known as the "Cockade City of the Union."

I enjoy stopping by this monument. It carries the names of all the officers and privates who served in the company, were wounded, killed in action, or were promoted, and it is surmounted by an American eagle of twenty-four karat gold. It did suffer serious damage from Federal cannonading during the Civil War. But it and its surrounding fences have been restored by the Cockade City Garden Club.

Major General William Phillips Memorial stone.

INTERESTING TOMBSTONES

Some tombstones of interesting people buried in the churchyard include:

The oldest tombstone in the cemetery belongs to Mrs. Rachel Williams, wife of Thomas Williams. She was born August 1735 in Gloucester, England and died July 23, 1746. One of her two daughters is buried in her grave.

The second oldest stone belongs to the second wife of Thomas Williams. She passed away July 25, 1747—two days later than the first wife and one year later (the, first wife being the 23rd of July, the second wife the 25th of July, a year apart).

Another interesting pair is A. McConnald and his wife. He passed away October 29, 1788, and she on November 2, 1788. Their tomb is just outside the church. Their son, Daniel, died at age two and is with them. Because McConnald was an English sailor, he is pictured in English sailor attire, and dying first, is leading his wife and son to Heaven. This historic stone was struck by a cannon ball during the siege of Petersburg and severed in two. It was spliced with an old hinge to restore it. No doubt, this was the only available material at the time.

One of the stories behind the graves in the cemetery concerned two men, Mr. Adams and Mr. Boisseau. Both became infatuated with a young woman, Miss Ellen Peniston, at a party, and fought a duel with pistols over her. Both men were shot and Doctor Iraira Smith, who attended them, later married Miss Ellen and the couple moved to Georgia.

A memorial was placed by the Ladies Memorial Association over the grave of Mrs. Nora Davidson, originator of Memorial Day on June 9. When I returned, June 9, 2014, to double-check on spellings, I also found the graves of Hiram Haines, his wife and family, along with Richard Rambaut with his wife and family. I have written about these people in the Hiram Haines Coffee Shop and Ale House chapter. I also discovered Charles O'Hara, who built Trapezium House, thanks to help from the church tour office.

There are many memorials to generals, historians, artists, physicians, governors, a baronet, and ministers of the Gospel. There are romantic tombs. Some are written to duelists. One even mentions a suicide, whose epitaph says: "Honor was his only vice." One old stone is shaped like a cradle, enclosed by a fence of marble slabs with a locked gate—though anyone can step over it easily.

Hiram Haines' grave.

An Investigation
MAY 31, 2014

I returned to the cemetery on Saturday, May 31, to conduct an EVP and ghost box session. Bill drove into the cemetery at 2 p.m. that afternoon and parked by the

The graves of Richard Rambaut and his wife.

curb, near the churchyard. I grabbed my recorder, camera, and the ghost box, hopped out of the car and stepped onto the drying, freshly cut grass. It had gotten warmer and a slight humidity filled the air. I switched on the recorder.

No one was around. That would make this easier to "talk" to the dead. A tombstone with McConnalds inscribed on the stone was nearby. I turned on the ghost box.

I asked, "Are the McConnalds here?"

A male voice answered:. "Aye. McConnald."

"What was the year you passed away?"

No reply.

"What did you die of?"

The man said, "Po—" I couldn't hear rest of the word due to static. What did he die of? Polio?

I turned to the next tombstone. It displayed two names: a married couple, Thomas Gateway Jones and Louise Burk.

"Is Thomas Jones or Louise here?"

A man said: "Yes. No." Did he mean yes to him being Thomas and no, Louise was not there?

"Can you tell me the year you died? I can see it on your stone here."

The man said: "What?"

"What, as what year you died? I just need the date of the year you passed away."
"18—" The rest went too low for me to catch. His gravestone did have 1813 as the year of his death.

I walked away and said aloud to anyone wanting to answer, "My name is Pamela. What is yours?"

Some voice blared over the scanning radio waves, but the static rose louder as well, so I turned off the ghost box and conducted a straight EVP session. Seeing a brick fenced area, I peeked over. A couple of headstones and three stone tables filled the spot, one of the tables broken in half. One of the tombstones had a cable wrapped around it, anchoring it to the stone, as it leaned over. I walked through the opening of the gate and stopped.

"Whoever this tombstone belongs to, can you tell me how you like that it is held up by cable? Did someone try to tip it over? Or was it something else, like a storm?" Later I learned I got nothing—neither voices or sounds out of the ordinary, just birds chirping or singing, and the sounds of a slight breeze. The name inscribed on the headstone was James and Isabella L. Dunlop. I turned to my right and saw on the other side of the gateway the gravestone of a Matilda Osborn. The inscription said she was born October 9, 1798, and had died four years later on December 22, 1802—not much of a life and just three days until Christmas when she passed away.

"Is Matilda still here? I should go out to my car as I have a ball that I bet you'd like to play with. Did you play with a ball when you were alive? Did you play with your friends?"

A young girl's voice replied: "Yes."

I asked two more questions: "Do you have a nanny and if so, what was her name?" But the little girl did not say anything else.

I left her alone and ambled over to a monument shaped like a gravestone. The inscription told about Major General Wm. (shortened for William) Philips. Supposedly, as mentioned before, his real grave was located near this location, though no one knew where. This monument was put up to acknowledge him.

With the ghost box on, I began to ask questions. "Major General Phillips? Is William Phillips here?"

A man's voice said, "Phillips!"

"I heard you were a British soldier. Are you buried nearby? Can you tell me?"
"Phillips. Can't."

I began to walk away. "Can you tell me if I am getting near where they buried you? Am I getting near?"

"No."

I wondered if he refused to tell me, or he didn't really know where he had been put into the ground.

"Major General Phillips, I see your name is William. My husband's name is William, too. What year did you die?"

"17—" was all I got. He had died in 1780.

"Did you die in the Revolutionary War?"

"Yes." I wasn't sure if this was him, or another ghost, as there were many gravestones from the 1700s in the churchyard and outside.

"By cannon fire or gunfire?"

"Gunfire."

"Who else is buried in this churchyard? Give me your name."

I got several names, though only two were distinguishable: "Philips.........Tap."

"How many spirits are with me? Are there more than five?"

A feminine voice said: "Five."

I didn't hear this at the time, but went on. "Is there more than ten?"

Nobody said anything to that one.

I wandered by a gravestone that displayed a man's name and that he'd died at age 64. I remarked, "I see you passed away at 64."

A male voice said, "Yes."

I turned off the ghost box and just left my recorder on, going into my spiel of them understanding they could not follow me home.

A soft feminine voice said, "Yes, yes, yes."

About ten minutes later, as I was talking, another female voice blared out, "Oh my Lord!" No one was around me and I hadn't said it. I wondered why this spirit uttered this.

Next time you think a cemetery is the last place for spirits to haunt, check out Blandford. The dead aren't quite dead in this cemetery. They're spirited.

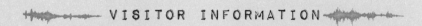

VISITOR INFORMATION

Blandford Church and Cemetery
111 Rochelle Lane
Petersburg, VA 23805
804-733-2396
www.petersburg-va.org/index.aspx?nid=393

Hours of operation are 10 a.m. to 4 p.m. Monday through Saturday, 12 p.m. to 4 p.m. on Sundays. Cemetery tours are offered throughout the year, including an extra Halloween evening tour on October 31.

DINWIDDIE

IF I HAD THE ENERGY, I WOULD HAVE DONE IT
ALL OVER THE COUNTY.

—EDWARD HOPPER

Paleo Indians prior to 8000 BC were the first residents of the area and it is thought they were nomadic hunter-gatherers following animal migrations. Early stone tools have been discovered in various fields within the county.

Dinwiddie was formed on May 1, 1752, having separated from Prince George County. The county is named for Robert Dinwiddie, Lieutenant Governor of Virginia, who served 1751 to 1758. Not long after that, the county raised several militia units for the American Revolution.

Dinwiddie County was the birth place of Elizabeth (Burwell) Hobbs Keckley. She was the free African-American dressmaker who worked for Mrs. Jefferson Davis, and later, she went to work for Mrs. Lincoln and became her close friend and confidante. Thomas Day was born in Dinwiddie, and he became well noted as a free African-American cabinetmaker in Milton, North Carolina, and southern Virginia. Another Dinwiddie native son, Dr. Thomas Stewart, is perhaps America's first free African-American eighteenth century rural physician.

The Civil War happened in Dinwiddie County as much as anywhere else in the Tri-Cities area. There are several Civil War battlefields, including

Historic Dinwiddie Courthouse. We drove to the historical Dinwiddie Courthouse after investigating Five Forks Battlefield. I did a quick ghost box session at the front doors and asked if any spirit still hung around there; a man's voice said: "General Pickett."

Dinwiddie Courthouse, Burgess Mill, Five Forks, Fort Gregg, Hatcher's Run, Lewis's Farm, Peebles' Farm, Ream's Station, Sutherland Station, The Breakthrough, Weldon Railroad, and White Oak Road. Two of the sites have museums: Five Forks, Pamplin Historical Park, and the National Museum of the Civil War Soldier.

The Dinwiddie County Courthouse became headquarters to Union General Philip H. Sheridan during the Battle of Dinwiddie Courthouse. The adjacent Calvary Episcopal Church was used as a hospital by the First Maine Cavalry. Ten unknown Union soldiers are buried in the churchyard. The courthouse was active through 1998. It is now home to the Dinwiddie County Historical Society and serves as a museum.

Dinwiddie is also known for other sights and events. At the Virginia Motorsports Park, one can watch drag races and, in August 2013, they actually had people run with the bulls like they do in Spain. The local fire department held a haunted forest in October 2013. The county holds a county fair every year, and there are parks and other recreational activities.

But more than that, it has many supernatural occurrences.

Central State Hospital

NO GREAT MIND HAS EVER EXISTED WITHOUT A TOUCH OF
MADNESS.

—ARISTOTLE

One of the older buildings of Central State Hospital.

It seems that hospitals, mental institutions, and old folks homes are the most logical places for hauntings. One of these is the Central State Hospital (CSH) located in Dinwiddie County, Virginia.

The origin of Central State Hospital dates back to the close of the Civil War. In April 1865, Congress created the Freedman's Bureau to establish hospitals, schools, and other facilities for the African-American population. A former Confederate facility, Howard's Grove Hospital, was designated as a mental health hospital for African-Americans in December 1869. Its name was later changed to Central Lunatic Asylum and, in June 1870, the General Assembly passed an act incorporating the Central Lunatic Asylum as an organized state institution. One hundred twenty-three insane persons and a hundred paupers considered not insane were housed at the asylum when the Commonwealth of Virginia took over.

Early institutional history notes that treatment at Central Lunatic Asylum during the 1890s was humane. Practices at the facility included seclusion, mechanical restraints, and the administering of hypnotics. Their definition of humane would include practices that today would be considered barbaric.

The Mayfield Farm in Dinwiddie County was purchased by the City of Petersburg for $15,000 in 1882. It was given to the Commonwealth and a total of 373 patients were transferred to the new hospital on March 22, 1885. The population doubled in ten years. By the end of 1950, 4,043 inpatients filled the place, though 691 were on parole or escape status. A few years later, the population reached 4,800. Overcrowding made patient safety a problem in some wards.

A Maximum Security Forensic Unit was built for the evaluation and treatment of patients referred by the courts. A geriatric treatment center was also erected for the care of the chronically ill and bedridden in the 1950s. The Barrow Geriatric Center was closed in the summer of 1985.

The years between 1962 and 1968 brought many changes to CSH with hospital services and facilities being upgraded, four adult treatment buildings erected, the beginning of treatment for adolescents, and the first alcohol abuse treatment program. From its founding until the passage of the Civil Rights Act of 1964, Central State Hospital served and treated only African-American mentally ill, mentally retarded, geriatric, and criminally insane from the entire state of Virginia. But in 1967, the place opened its doors to all patients regardless of race or national origin, but only from the Central Virginia area.

Ghost Stories

Now for the ghost stories about the place: There are those who say noises are heard and an apparition has been seen in the hallways of one of the older buildings. An oppressive or foreboding feeling has been felt while on the property. Sounds of heavy footsteps are heard and small balls of light that dart about the property are seen. One tale told is about a young woman and her friends going to the location. They caught a very disturbing photo of an apparition surrounded in multi-colored orbs. This picture was taken as they left, just as they heard a loud female scream coming from the courtyard area.

The historic structure has been replaced by a modern building. The old buildings were empty. Developmental Disabilities (DD) waivers were made for the living residents to be transferred elsewhere. I am not sure, but I assume the spirits that haunt this building will remain to stalk the halls. Though I couldn't investigate the inside, Bill and I did drive through the property. We found a mixture of old buildings and modern ones on quite a few acres. None of the photos I took had anything supernatural in them.

Hospitals, mental institutions, and prisons are great places for paranormal activity long after they are closed. Central State Hospital is proof it can be a paranormal hotspot while opened, too.

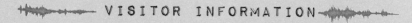

VISITOR INFORMATION

Central State Hospital (CSH)
26317 W. Washington Street
Petersburg, VA 23803
804-524-7000
www.csh.dbhds.virginia.gov

Central State Hospital and its land are private property, and I ask that no one go there to conduct a paranormal investigation. You will be arrested. I have seen people post online that they have asked to investigate there and were not given permission. I did not attempt to do this at all—but just drove on the roads, took a couple of pictures, and then left.

Special Note: Remember that in any investigation you conduct, especially at night (but even daytime, too, for privately owned places), get the owner's permission. Never go on private land to investigate.

Petersburg National Civil War Battlefield —Five Forks

WAR IS HELL.
— GENERAL WILLIAM T. SHERMAN

Spot 3, where Colonel William R. J. Peagram died.

The Battle of Five Forks, the last major battle of the Petersburg Campaign during the War Between the States, occurred on April 1, 1865. It is called "The Waterloo of the Confederacy." By defeating Confederate infantry under George E. Pickett and cavalry under William H. F. "Rooney" Lee, Fitzhugh Lee, and Thomas L. Rosser, Union General Philip H. Sheridan was able to flank the Confederate lines at Petersburg. The action allowed the Union Army, after nearly ten months of siege, to break through Confederate General Robert E. Lee's lines and, by April 2, they were able to claim Petersburg and the Confederate capital in Richmond. With Union troops positioned along the major south transportation routes, they forced evacuating Confederate troops to travel west during the Appomattox

Campaign. As good history buffs know, after the battle at Sailor's Creek, where the Confederates lost, Robert E. Lee surrendered at the Appomattox Courthouse.

The Five Forks battle caused major implications in two careers. When the fighting began, Pickett was famously absent behind the lines at a shad bake. He failed to coordinate the action properly and stained his reputation. Union General Gouverneur K. Warren was relieved of command during the battle, a move by Sheridan that was ruled improper in 1879.

These movements cultivated a battle that began on March 29, 1865. Union General Ulysses S. Grant continued his strategy of stretching Union lines farther and farther to the Union's left. This forced Confederate General Robert E. Lee to extend his lines to the breaking point. Grant shifted his forces of 54,500 infantry and 13,000 cavalry at Petersburg to concentrate on Lee's right. The Union Fifth Corps, under the command of Gouverneur K. Warren, took the far left flank. Sheridan's cavalry corps swung to the far west and prepared to strike toward Dinwiddie Courthouse. From there, they moved north and severed the Danville and the South Side Railroad. This was the last remaining supply line for Lee's Army of Northern Virginia and the other Confederate troops in the entrenchments around Richmond and Petersburg.

Griffin's division of the Fifth Corps clashed with units on the Confederate far right at Lewis Farm on March 29. The action pushed the Confederates back. Feeling victory close at hand, this made Grant more determined to convert Sheridan's proposed raid into a full-fledged flanking maneuver, which Lee attempted to block. The only troops available to blunt the Union advance were the infantry division of George E. Pickett and the cavalry divisions of Rooney Lee, Fitz Lee, and Thomas Rosser. Under the command of Pickett, they marched westward and arrived at Five Forks the afternoon of March 30, 1865.

Two battles happened on March 31, 1865, that set the stage for Five Forks. The Battle of Dinwiddie Courthouse developed between Sheridan's cavalry and Pickett's task force and lasted until nightfall. Opposing scouts met at Dinwiddie Courthouse. Sheridan and Pickett fed more troops into the fight. Pickett commanded the Confederate side of the encounter well, but he still failed to defeat Sheridan. The second engagement was along White Oak Road. It involved units on Lee's far right near Burgess's Mill and Hatcher's Run, and Union troops from the Fifth Corps and the Second Corps. No matter how hard they fought, the tenuous link between Pickett's exposed men near Five Forks and the bulk of the Army of Northern Virginia had been severed. Lee's flank had been turned. Grant had cut off Pickett's force.

Pickett withdrew his troops back from Dinwiddie Courthouse on the morning of April 1, 1865, and headed for the vicinity of Five Forks. That afternoon, Confederate Generals George E. Pickett, Thomas L. Rosser, and Fitzhugh Lee left their commands to enjoy a shad bake. There are stories that maybe the Confederate leaders also imbibed a tipple of whiskey along with their fish. They also neglected to inform their subordinates where they might be found. When the Union assault struck, they could not be located. Pickett returned to the field to watch his lines dissolve under Union pressure, too late to salvage anything. By seven that night, the Union had driven the Confederates from the field.

The Battle of Five Forks rendered the Confederate position at Petersburg and Richmond untenable. Sheridan and the Fifth Corps sat poised to cut off the supply line of the South Side Railroad, and they occupied a position from which they could attempt to cut off the Army of Northern Virginia's line of retreat from a flight westward. Sheridan's removal of Warren lasted far beyond the end of the war, as he had ended Warren's military career. Warren did try and pressed for a formal court of inquiry to review Sheridan's decision to relieve him. Warren got his review in 1879. Sheridan had been charged with acting improperly, and the verdict rendered nothing more than a moral victory to Warren by that late date.

An Investigative Tour

Bill and I took the Five Forks driving tour on Saturday, July 5, 2014. It was a nice sunny day with no humidity. Besides the visitor's center, there were five spots to stop on the tour. The whole of the Five Forks Battlefield is at the intersection of the White Oak Road, Scott's Road, Ford's Road, and the Dinwiddie Courthouse Road. I conducted an EVP and ghost box session at each of the five. I did use my EMF meter, but obtained nothing at any of the locations.

Spot 1: Courthouse Road and the Visitor Center

At Spot 1, just before the Visitor Center and on Courthouse Road, we pulled in the parking lot. I got out with the EMF meter, recorder, and ghost box. Turning on the recorder, I noted the date and time, did a short EVP session, followed by using the ghost box. (This would be the same process at each of the other four spots.)

When I asked if anyone was at Spot 1, I got a "Me."

I asked, "Spirits?"

Once again: "Me."

I asked for a name and got "Roc." It sounded like "Roc," and I assumed not "rock" or anything else.

I asked if he was Federal or Confederate. A question of how many of Pickett's men might still be at Five Forks got me what sounded like "fifty." Of Union, the reply of "sixty" was received.

When I asked if he had been part of Pickett's bunch, he answered with a "Yes."

Not getting much more, we got back on Courthouse Road, to go to our next destination.

Spot 2: White Oak Road

Before we headed to Spot 2, we stopped by the Visitor Center, so I could grab a map of the battlefield and the both of us could use the restroom. Within fifteen minutes, we were back on Courthouse Road and turned right on to White Oak Road. We saw the small parking lot for Spot 2 to our left. Unfortunately, this spot proved futile after fifteen minutes of not getting anything on my ghost box, plus not one EVP on my recorder.

Spot 3: White Oak Road

Bill drove down White Oak Road, crossed through the intersection, then turned right to pull into the parking lot of Spot 3. There were two fields on each side of White Oak Road. I crossed the street to the one with the cannon and part of a fence saying "Pegram." The story states that Colonel William R. J. Pegram was tending to his artillery when Sheridan's forces arrived in the area, on the afternoon of April 1, 1865, and attacked. Warren's infantry swept down from the east. After the fierce fighting, the Confederate positions around the intersection collapsed. During the melee, Pegram fell, mortally wounded. At age twenty-three, he died just five miles short of his ancestral home and nine days short of the war ending, after surviving many of the Army of Northern Virginia's battles.

On a short EVP session, all I got was "David." Someone else who fell at the battle here? Which side?

My ghost box got a few more responses. When I asked Pegram to say "Willie" on my ghost box, a male voice replied with "Box?" Then I heard "Angel." I asked if the reason Pegram wasn't there was because he was an angel now; a voice said: "Yes."

I crossed back over to the field with the monuments to take some pictures and to read what was written on them, before I headed back to the Spot 3 parking lot where Bill waited in the car. We left to drive down the road to Spot 4.

Spot 4: Final Battle on White Oak Road

Spot 4 designated where the final battle happened during the siege led by General George Armstrong Custer. On the land one can find the Gilliam house, better known as Burnt Quarter, which has its own ghost (in the chapter, "Spooky Tales of Dinwiddie County"). The only anomalies I received came from my ghost box. When I'd asked what they would like me to tell my readers for this book, a man said, "Shoot first." What did he mean, or did he mean anything? I said goodbye and thanked them for any answers. A man replied, "Thank you." Death obviously did not end their politeness. I got in the car and we left. Bill drove us to the last spot.

Spot 5: Ford Road

We arrived at the fifth and last part of the tour on Ford Road. When I hadn't gotten any answers about the War Between the States, I decided to switch tactics and asked if anything from the Revolution or War of 1812 happened at this spot. A man's voice came over the box: "Pickett." Okay, now a Civil War spirit decided to say something. Pickett was here in the battle. Was it Pickett who told me his name or one of his men who has fallen in battle? I asked for a last name after introducing mine and I got "Kent." Maybe it was one of Pickett's men?

The last stop before heading home for Chesterfield was the historical Dinwiddie Courthouse. What I got there on my ghost box is with the photo of the building in the Dinwiddie chapter.

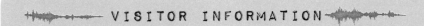

VISITOR INFORMATION

Petersburg National Civil War Battlefield: Five Forks
9840 Courthouse Road
Petersburg, VA 23803

Five Forks Battlefield is located at the intersections of White Oak Road, Scott's Road, Ford's Road, and the Dinwiddie Courthouse Road.

Petersburg National Battlefield Headquarters
1539 Hickory Hill Road
Petersburg, VA 23803-4721
804-732-3531
www.nps.gov/pete/historyculture/five-forks.htm

There is a Visitor Contact Station that opened in 2009. It is open seven days a week from 9 a.m. to 5 p.m. with the exception of certain holidays. The Visitor Contact Station includes museum displays, artifacts, and a twelve-minute video. There is a picnic pavilion and an eight-mile trail system just outside of the station.

In addition to their website shown above, for more information, check out their Facebook page at www.facebook.com/PetersburgNPS. For a map of where the five spots and Visitor's Center are located see the website above.

Poplar Grove National Cemetery

THE WING OF THE FALCON BRINGS TO THE KING, THE
WING OF THE CROW BRING HIM TO THE CEMETERY.

—MUHAMMED IQBAL

Gates of Poplar Cemetery.

Poplar Grove National Cemetery is located at 8005 Vaughan Road in Dinwiddie County. Union Army soldiers are buried here, and the cemetery was maintained by the War Department until 1933, when the National Park Service (NPS) took over. It is one of fourteen national cemeteries cared for by NPS.

During the siege, Union soldiers killed in battle were hastily buried in the ground where the fighting took place. Some ended up in single, shallow pits, others in mass graves. Identification was simplified as a name carved on a wooden headboard, if time allowed. Some units, like the IX Corps, had small cemeteries near their filled hospitals for soldiers who died while in their care.

Lieutenant Colonel James Moore began his survey of the Petersburg area, in 1866, to locate land for a National Cemetery. A farm just south of the city was chosen as the new residence. This tract of land had been the campground for the 50th New York Volunteer Engineers. During the war, they constructed a Gothic-style, pine-log church called Poplar Grove.

Five thousand Union soldiers were taken from nearly a hundred separate burial sites around Petersburg, while other bodies were moved from nine Virginia counties. All this was accomplished by a hundred men who made up the "burial troops." Remains were placed in plain wooden coffins with headboards attached, if available. The burial corps worked for three years, until 1869, reinterring 6,718 remains. Only 2,139 bodies were positively identified. It was the same for those 30,000 buried at Blandford Church Cemetery—only 2,000 names known. Soldiers from other wars were also buried at Poplar. When Bill and I went there May 25, 2014, in the afternoon, he felt sure he saw one for the Korean War, but none later than that. Two Medal of Honor recipients are buried there: Lewis Morgan and Henry Hardenburg. I also saw a grave from World War I.

Today, you won't see gravestones for Civil War soldiers (and the others, either); you will only see plagues on the graves. Because Petersburg needed money in the 1930s, they sold the tombstones to a builder who created a house and walkway with them. (The house has its own chapter in this book.)

I'd been to this cemetery before while I was writing *Haunted Richmond II*. On their website, they stated the cemetery was open 365 days a year from dawn to dusk; however, on that Friday, in January 2011, the gates were locked and no one was around. I almost passed the road that led to the cemetery, even with GPS coordinates, so if you plan to visit the place, keep your eyes peeled for the sign.

Though I got nothing from EVPs, there had been a couple of positive photos. One of them had mist and yet, it was a clear, sunny day—just cold. You can see the shot in *Haunted Richmond II*.

When I returned with Bill, it was in the high 70s and sunny. He broke off to wander around, and I settled under a tree where an unknown Civil War soldier lay buried. All I got in the regular recordings were the birds singing and chirping, the breeze, Bill and I talking, and the roar of the occasional vehicle driving up to the parking lot or from the nearby road. The ghost box did get a few voices answering me, though.

Ghost Box Sessions

I asked if the unknown Civil War soldier was there with me, and his name. A man answered: "Nick."

I asked, "Last name? What battle did you die in?"

No answer.

"Union?"

The same male voice came over the box: "Union."

I asked, "How many spirits are with me?"

A different male voice: "Six."

"North or South?" I asked this three times, before I got an answer. A man with a deeper male voice said: "North."

I tried for the unknown soldier's name again, and a male voice came from the box with: "Bip..." When I asked for it again, I got the same answer of "Bip.." ...At least it sounded like that.

I said, "What is your rank?"

"Lieutenant."

I broke off the conversation and said goodbye. Switching off the ghost box, I left my recorder on to catch any EVPs as I went to find Bill.

Before we left for home, I walked over to the family cemetery and tried a ghost box session there. I noticed two headstones with both the husband and wife's names on each. The one against the fence revealed "Jones." The other to my left had "Odom." I did catch the women's names: Rebecca Odom and Nellie Jones.

I asked, "Anybody here?"

Woman answered: "No."

"What is your name?"

"O..." Didn't catch the rest—"O" for Odam?

"Nellie Jones. Is Nellie Jones here?"

A soft woman's voice said: "Yes."

"So, there are spirits here?"

A man blurted out, "No!"

"You're saying, neither from this family cemetery or from Poplar Grove, no spirits at all?"

The man's voice again: "No."

I guess they didn't want me bugging them, so I said goodbye and joined my husband in the car to head for home.

Next time, you go to the Poplar Grove National Cemetery, don't be surprised if you catch the phantoms of a few soldiers hanging around. Just tell them thanks for their service.

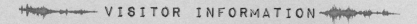 **VISITOR INFORMATION**

Poplar Grove National Cemetery
8005 Vaughan Road
Petersburg, VA 23805
www.nps.gov/pete/learn/historyculture/poplar-grove-national-cemetery.htm

Sutherland Tavern

I DEFINITELY BELIEVE IN GHOSTS.

— JENNA DEWAN

Sutherland Tavern.

Sutherland's Tavern, also known as Fork's Inn, served as the first US Post Office in the area, a Civil War hospital, an inn, and a tavern. Today, the period-furnished home is open twice a year to the public: in the fall for the Ghost and Spirit Tour and in early spring for the Southside Virginia Heritage Days.

The house was built in 1803. The owner, Fendall Sutherland, ran it as a tavern. He is buried in the family cemetery and died in 1833. With this tavern, he could get the business coming from the stagecoaches that passed through town. He also had a restaurant in the building and kept the property as a working plantation with sixteen slaves he owned. The family graveyard is still at the back of the house beneath a tree, but the current owners, the Olgers, do not know where the slave cemetery is located.

The Battle of Sutherland Station happened literally on the front lawn of this property on April 2, 1865. The building became a Union hospital, where soldiers were arranged on the parlor floor head to toe. Many died as the battle raged on.

In 1873, the Sutherland who owned the place then, sold it to the Myers of New Jersey. One of their children, Joel, passed away before they moved back to New Jersey. He is buried outside the family cemetery as being a Northerner; the locals did not want him buried inside the sanctioned ground.

The Myers sold the place to the Olgers in 1903. It has been in the new family ever since. Since 1903, many Olgers died in the house, too, and are buried in a fenced-in area in the backyard.

The house consists of fourteen rooms that are furnished with a large and diverse collection of late eighteenth- and early-nineteenth century furnishings that one would expect to find in a Virginia plantation home. The collection ranges from a large variety of early clocks to coin silver, early lighting, paintings, and a collection of Civil War artifacts and weapons from the Battle of Sutherland Station. Many of the artifacts have been donated from families in the Petersburg and Dinwiddie area.

Darrell Olgers restored the more than 200-year-old family home and former tavern, living there along with his wife, Michelle, and daughter, Emma. They enjoy the period furniture and art, each of which has its own story, from the mantle pieces of a King George County home that once shared a room with a wounded John Wilkes Booth, to the long case clock, where Olgers hid his wife's engagement ring.

Ghost Tour:
OCTOBER 20, 2013

I learned that the Olgers opened their home for ghost tours in October 2013. A friend posted information about the tours on the Richmond Paranormal Society Facebook group. I thought I'd missed them, but lucky for me, they decided to hold one last tour on Sunday, October 20, 2013. I called and reserved a couple of spots for my husband Bill and me. After the tour, master storyteller Jimmy Olgers would be recounting ghost stories associated with Dinwiddie County by the firelight in the old cooking kitchen where many of the sixteen slaves at Sutherland's Tavern, in 1834, would have worked.

The Olgers family's personal experiences and haunting tales of others' experiences in the house throughout the years were told, such as unexplained noises and pacing footsteps that quickened during thunderstorms. Michelle Olgers passed around an eerie image taken by paranormal investigators of a "presence" in the home that remains unexplained. It stood at the parlor window nearest to the front door. After an attempt of three photos taken outside of the windows, the investigators found a figure in the third one.

Michelle told the tour group of a wedding between two reenactors during the Southside Virginia Heritage Days (a special event held every spring). The woman discovered a white face looking out of the same window just mentioned in a photo she had taken! Another photo Michelle showed came from their daughter's bedroom. There appeared to be a black cat in the picture with a creepy face. They have a brown and white cat that they keep locked up during the tours, so they knew it wasn't their cat. It was later at The Bistro at Market and Grove that I found that it had been Russ Johnson from The Bistro who had taken the photograph.

Michelle began the official tour, giving us a bit of history about why she had a coffin on the table in the parlor. In the past, parlors were where people placed their dead after they'd passed away. In fact, parlors had been called death rooms once upon a time. The body was laid out for two to five days: one day was needed to put out the call about the death, another couple of days were for people to gather there, and a couple of more days were needed for viewing the body. This was called a "wake."

Today, people bring flowers to give the families of the deceased. This, too, had to do with the body in the parlor. It began to smell, so placing many flowers in the parlor helped tone down the stench. Also, all clocks in the house were stopped, and any mirrors covered. Clocks were stopped at the hour of the death of the person laid out. Superstition had them believing that if they were not stopped, the living would have bad luck. There were also superstitions regarding mirrors: covering them wherever the dead were laid out was to prevent disembodied spirits from seeing their own reflections and never finding rest. Other reasons stated that mirrors should be covered so the soul of the departed wouldn't get caught behind the glass and be unable to pass to the other side. There is one final belief that if the living saw their own reflection in a mirror while a body lay in the parlor, they would die soon after. The pallbearers carried the body out the front door feet first, so not to beckon any souls back into the house.

OTHER INTERESTING SUPERSTITIONS ABOUT DEATH

There are other interesting superstitions concerning death.

- It is bad luck to meet a funeral procession head on. If you see one approaching, turn around. If this is unavoidable, hold on to a button until the funeral cortege passes.
- When a clap of thunder is heard following a burial, it is an indication that the soul of the departed has reached heaven.
- Do not hold your breath while going by a graveyard, so you will not be buried.
- If the deceased has lived a good life, flowers will bloom on his grave; but if he has been evil, only weeds will grow.
- The odor of roses when no one is around indicates that someone will die.
- Seeing yourself in a dream means that your death will follow.
- If a sparrow lands on a piano, someone in the home will die.
- A picture falling off a wall means that there will be a death of someone you know.
- A single snowdrop growing in the garden foretells death.

In the Victorian times, one had much to worry about when it concerned death, or the death of a loved one!

When Abraham Lincoln became the first famous person embalmed, funeral homes were established. No one called parlors death rooms after that; instead, they became known as living rooms, as the living used them.

Darrell led us into the room across the hall from the parlor. He pointed at a painting on the wall of a lady in a white dress with dark hair in ringlets. In another tour, a man had seen the portrait and asked if the "lady" would be conducting the tour as he had seen her looking out from an upstairs window. Olgers told the man that she wouldn't be giving tours because she was dead. That man quickly opted out of the tour and left.

This was not the first time people had seen the ghost lady. One lady stopped Darrell Olgers at the local Food Lion and told him that when she drove by the house, she saw a woman in white looking out the upstairs window and wondered who she was.

A few years ago, Emma arrived home from school one afternoon. She was upstairs watching television when she heard a loud slam of the front door downstairs. She went to the top of the stairs and watched as the door opened and slammed shut, then repeated the action. Frightened, she grabbed her father's nine millimeter gun before she went downstairs to check the place out.

Olgers pointed at the painting and said, "Go ahead and take pictures of the portrait. Several people have reported finding a strange glow around it in their photographs."

I didn't get anything on my photos of her that night. No one else said if they did, either.

Olgers called out, "Give us a sign that you are with us tonight."

Nothing happened live. Later, I listened to my recording to find I hadn't any EVPs of the lady or anyone else answering him.

Olgers led us upstairs. He took us into his daughter's bedroom. I said, "If there are any spirits in this room, talk into the recorder that I am holding." All of a sudden, a wave of heat swept over me, and I remarked on it. Olgers said that several people admitted to feeling hot in this room, more than anywhere else in the house. (I do feel hot a lot, so it may be due to something *not* supernatural in my case.)

He went right into what spirits had been seen in his daughter's room. The first story began when his daughter was much younger and of her waking them in the night with her screaming. When they ran in, she told them that every night she would awaken to a tall figure dressed in a black coat with a top hat standing at the foot of her bed. She never saw his face, just swirling smoke where his face should be.

Darrell pointed at a framed sampler in the room. It had been done by a young girl in Lindenburg County in 1790. She'd died at age ten. Emma would see the ghost of the girl standing in front of the sampler, but only in the fall.

"Are you Mary Ellen?" she'd asked one time.

The phantom dissipated. After that, Emma never said anything that might scare the ghost away. She just watched her.

Olgers took us to another room and talked about how people entering it felt breath on their necks, their hair pulled, and one woman fell to the floor in a faint from something overcoming her. Nothing happened to me, however, and none of the others remarked about anything unusual.

We entered the master bedroom. Darrell showed us the window where the woman in white would be seen looking out. He told us that when he first moved to the house in 1996, he had an episode of disembodied footsteps pacing back and forth in front of him in another part of the second floor. Another time, he hired someone to paint the walls. The man could only do it at night. He heard footsteps from upstairs all through the night. He didn't return the next night.

Another time, a psychic asked if his house was haunted. Darrell replied, "You're the psychic; you tell me." She climbed the stairs to the second floor to enter the main bedroom and turned around to say, "There is a couple here. The woman is smiling, and is short and plump with wavy hair. The man has a mustache and is stern-looking, and he is fond of his bowler hat." Darrell recognized his great-grandparents from the description.

After a bit, we followed Darrell downstairs and out the front door where he led us around the house to the cemetery in the back yard. I snapped pictures along the way. Though nothing happened out of the ordinary during the tour, I still had the feeling of being watched. Darrell talked about the cemetery, pointing out Joel Myer's grave, and he told the story of why he was not allowed to be buried inside the Sutherland family plot. When he told us the tour was over and to head for the kitchen where Jimmy Olgers would tell us some ghost stories of Dinwiddie, I remained and began an EVP session at the graves.

I asked, "Are any of the Civil War soldiers who died in the battle that happened here with me tonight?"

I pointed to the graves. "There is a fence around one of the graves. Was this because that person was special to the Sutherlands?"

Then I asked, "Are you still with us, Joel?"

Later, as I listened to the recording at home, a male voice yelled: "Hey!" I didn't hear it out loud, but the recorder picked it up. I thought back to remember if anyone had been around, but I had been the only one there at the time. Who had said this? One of the Sutherlands, maybe Joel? A Civil War soldier? An Olgers who had passed away? Surely it was Joel, as I had just asked him a question beforehand and was near his grave.

Sadly, that was the only EVP I caught that night. I wished I had gotten more, but that is the way it goes sometimes. Participating in a ghost tour makes it hard to conduct a ghost box session.

After the storytelling in the kitchen, everyone headed for their vehicles. I shot more pictures in front of the house, particularly the parlor window that had been known to show figures and faces in photos. One close-up of the ghost tour sign got some anomaly of lines. In another part of the house, I took as the last picture while standing by my car; I caught a shadowy figure looking out one of the windows in that last photo. No family member was in the living room at the time, and Bill and I the only ones left from the tour.

Close-up of the living room window to the left that reveals a shadowy figure peeking out the window. No one living was in the room at the time. All but Bill and I remained from the last tour, as the rest had already left.

Interview and Investigation
JUNE 17, 2014

It was close to 7 p.m. on the Tuesday I arrived to do a further interview with the Olgers and an investigation. I walked up the path to the front porch and knocked at the front door that had been used for those taking the October ghost tour. Darrell Olgers stepped out from a door to my far left and told me to come to that one.

Once inside, he gestured at the kitchen table where his daughter Emma, his wife Michelle, and he sat. I got out a recorder, turned it on, and sat down to begin the interview portion. Darrell mentioned the experience he'd had with the entity that walked back and forth on the second floor in one hallway, acting like it was agitated. (I remembered this from the ghost tour in October.)

Darrell felt that the ghost hated thunderstorms, as that is when its footsteps are heard. They appeared to grow more intense as the storm worsened. One time, the whole family went to read in a room off the hallway because it was the coldest room in the house. It began to thunder, and he'd heard the footsteps start. Hoping to see the spirit, he'd thrown open the door and the security light outside lit up the hallway—but he saw nothing.

He also mentioned a lady ghost with long dark hair. She was always seen by people at the window on the second floor.

Michelle never had anything supernatural happen to her, usually because the spirits liked her or they didn't like her. The spookiest thing she came closest to experiencing was when Emma was little. Michelle was washing dishes in one room, but Emma kept staring into another room and asking, "Who's that?" Three times she did this and three times Michelle went to look, but saw nothing. It still gave her the chills.

Eleven-year-old Emma has had a few more experiences of her own since the ghost tour. One concerned the figure in the top hat and dark coat with no face she'd encountered when younger. The phantom had disappeared for a long while, but had returned lately to haunt her. This time, not satisfied with just standing at the foot of her bed to stare at her, he began to follow her around the house.

Before she and her parents were about to leave for the June Friday of the Arts, Emma remembered she had forgotten her phone. She rushed upstairs to grab it. Her cat leaped up behind her in the room, so she picked the feline up to carry it downstairs with her. As she passed her parent's bedroom, she saw a black figure inside. At first, she thought she'd imagined it, but her cat went freaky and kept staring inside the room for no reason.

She thought, *It's only a dark shirt.* When she tried to find that dark shirt, she didn't find one anywhere.

Later, as she took me around for my investigation, she mentioned two other things that had happened to her. When she'd walked down a hallway, she'd heard a growl—loud and clear—but saw nothing. That really scared her. Another time, she saw a woman in a dress from what looked like the Civil War era. The ghost kept beckoning to her as though she wanted Emma to follow.

Another story Emma told me had a girl visiting the house. This girl was sent downstairs to be alone. Suddenly, Emma and her parents heard a scream and they rushed downstairs to find her crying and yelling about something grabbing her.

Emma also told me something that happened to her aunt when she was a young girl. As her aunt played in the first floor hallway near the staircase, she saw something in the shape of a basketball float down the stairs, only to vanish.

We left Darrell and Michelle, and Emma opened the door and led me to the living room to begin the investigation. This was the room where the ghost tour had commenced and where I had caught that picture of someone looking out of the window near the door to the kitchen that night in October. I began the ghost box session as my recorder had been recording since the interview.

I said, "Are there any spirits with us?"

A woman's voice came over the box: "Yes." She had been so soft spoken that I hadn't heard her at that time over the scanning. I discovered her answering me when I listened to the recording at home the next day.

A man spoke up after her: "Yes."

"Who is here with us? I heard a gentleman." Maybe the same male voice said something, but it was too low to catch the words.

"Can I have your name?" A man said something like "three" or "Lee." The static made it hard to tell.

"Can you speak louder?"

Emma wondered if her great-great-grandfather was in the room with us. I asked, "Is Emma's great-great-grandfather here?"

"Yes."

"To be sure it is you, can you say Emma's name?"

Nothing.

"My name is Pamela."

I heard again what I'd heard in the living room, either "three" or "Lee." It occurred to me, that maybe the ghost was telling me to leave, and not saying what I'd thought.

We walked to the hallway. "Who is with us?"

I got a man's voice across the box: "It's me."

"Name, please?"

"Please."

Was I being mocked? Not once had I heard a radio station come on across the waves since I started the session inside the house. That rarely happens.

I saw the closed door across from the staircase and asked Emma if it was locked. She said, "No, it's not." So we opened the door and went inside. Some kind of odor filled the air. It dissipated within a couple of seconds after we closed the door behind us. I couldn't think of what it smelled like. I knew that odor was not there when we'd entered the room during the ghost tour. Had the spirits caused it? Whatever the scent, it never came back during our session there or when we left.

"Is the lady here? I smelled something in the room when I first walked in. Now it is gone."

Emma pointed at the portrait of the lady hanging on the wall above the couch. I snapped a couple of shots of it. Emma said her name was Miss Tyler.

I asked, "Is Miss Tyler here?"

No answer.

I asked again. "Is Miss Tyler here?"

Nothing.

Portrait of Miss Tyler. Her spirit has been seen looking out an upstairs bedroom window.

We left the room and climbed the stairs to the second floor. I asked Emma at the top what her great-great-grandfather's name might be. She wasn't sure, but she thought it might be John Benjamin.

"John Benjamin here?"

"Huh?"

"Is your name John?"

"Hugh." Who was Hugh?

I held my camera in my free hand. "You could be in a picture."

The man again: "Maybe."

Emma led me through a bathroom to walk down a hall to her bedroom.

Once inside, I said, "Anybody here? Is the little girl here? The one connected to the framed needlepoint?"

Emma said, "Her name is Mary Ellen."

I said, "Is Mary Ellen here?"

I didn't get a girl's voice across the ghost box. I tried something else.

"Who is the gentleman with the top hat and dark coat Emma has seen in here? Can you tell me your name?"

A man with a deep voice spoke: "No."

"Is this Emma' grandfather?"

"No."

"Civil War soldiers here? Anybody?"

"Me."

"Who is with us?"

The same guy again. The voice sounded the same: "Me."

"Give me your name?"

A female voice: "No." A male one: "No."

"Did I hear John?"

"No."

"Who has been haunting this room over the years?"

"We have..." Static overcame what else was being said.

The scanning quit. I restarted it.

Emma led me to her parent's bedroom next. I left my second recorder on and lay it on the dresser in Emma's bedroom, hoping I might catch some EVPs during the time we were in the other bedroom.

Emma opened the door and said, "Good grief!"

A voice piped up on my box: "Yep."

I noticed the Confederate outfit by the door and felt the coolness from the AC unit behind the rocking chair. Emma suggested maybe the ghosts could move the curtains.

"Can you move the curtains in the window where the lady has been seen?"

Nothing moved.

"Is the lady here? Miss Tyler?"

She did not answer me.

"Can Miss Tyler speak?"

A man said: "No."

"Can she speak?"

A man said: "Ma'am?"

I asked Emma to shut off the AC so we could have quiet (something I should have done earlier). I shut off the box and did a straight EVP session. Emma settled on the bed, and as I looked at the rocking chair across the room, I saw it rock once, then stop.

"I saw the rocking chair move. Did you get out of it? You can sit in it. We don't mind."

The chair didn't move, though. I asked a few more questions before we left the room to head back to Emma's.

Later as I listened, I heard an EVP of footsteps coming from outside the room in the hallway. The other recorder I had left in Emma's bedroom also captured the same footsteps.

Emma suggested taking a photo of the corner where someone else had captured a cat in a photo they took. I took several. I paused after snapping, as I thought I saw something in one of them. I clicked back to that picture and saw a shadow at the bottom of the dollhouse.

I asked, "Do you like the dollhouse? Who made the shadow at the bottom of the dollhouse? Is it the little girl?"

A male voice came across the box: "P....l..."

I said, "Can I speak to the little girl? No?" I asked three times before I got an answer.

It came from a man and not the little girl. "Huh?"

"What do you mean, huh? Is it all men today?"

The man said, "No, but..."

Shadow at the bottom of the dollhouse in Emma Olger's bedroom.

"No, but what?" Was it hard for him to give the complete sentence? "Are you the one who is the shadow in my picture? Yes or no." "It's me."

"Thank you for being in my photograph." I gathered my stuff and moved toward the doorway. "We're going to another part of the house. Goodbye."

Emma followed. "Goodbye."

The man asked: "Why?"

"Because you don't appear to want to talk to me. So, goodbye."

Except for the static and scanning sounds, no one answered us.

We headed to the other side of the house where Darrell had heard the pacing footsteps. I saw doors to two bedrooms off the hallway, peered in one, and then took a picture. Freezing cold air wafted from the other room when I opened its door, making me shiver.

Emma explained, "That is the coldest room in the house. When you want to get away from the heat, it is the perfect place."

I turned the ghost box back on. "I hear there is someone here who paces from one end of the hall and back during a thunderstorm. The footsteps appear to sound more agitated as the thunderstorm grows worse. Who is it?"

Nothing.

I tried again. "Were you here last week when the storms hit bad? If you need help to be able to communicate, use my energy to assist you."

A man's voice came across the box: "Huh?"

"Are you the one who paces back and forth in this hallway?"

"Me."

"Do the storms bother you?"

"What?"

Looking out the window that had a broken piece of glass in the bottom pane, I saw the front lawn of the house and the memorial for the Battle of Sutherland Station. I remembered this building had been used as a Union hospital.

I asked, "Are you a Civil War soldier? Do those storms remind you of the battle that happened here?"

A man said: "Drum." Another said: "Right."

"What is your name?"

"Ben." I heard this off the recording in real time, though Emma thought he said Benjamin (her great-great-grandfather's name). This voice sounded younger, and I wondered if a soldier had died in the house when it was used as a hospital or during the battle outside.

"Do you follow Emma around the house? Watch over her? Make sure she's okay? She's a lady of the South."

"No."

"What is your last name?"

"Pope."

"Did you visit it when it was Fork Inn?"

"No." Another male voice: "Fork..." Maybe this other man meant Fork Inn and that he had visited it.

"Is Mr. Sutherland who built the tavern here? Are you still around the house?"

"No."

"Pope." No doubt, Ben Pope meant to press home he was with us. Though was that Ben Pope or another guy?

We thanked them for whatever they gave us and clattered downstairs to the kitchen where Emma's parents waited. I told them what I might have gotten with the ghost box and showed the photo with the shadow. I then told them I would investigate the cemeteries and the location of the battle before I drove home.

Emma followed me out and to the Sutherland family cemetery. I went to Joel Myers' grave first.

"Soon as the ghost box came on, a man called out from it: "Hello?"

"Are you here, Joel?"

"Huh?" This was the same voice that said hello.

"Is Joel Myers here?"

A boy's voice said: "Huh?"

"Back in October, I was here and got a recording of a boy saying, 'Hey!' after I'd asked if Joel was still around. Was that you?"

"Yes."

"Are you upset not being buried in the Sutherland family cemetery?"

"Yes."

"I am going to the Sutherlands' graves. You can follow us, Joel."

"No." Did the other spirits make it hard for him to cross into their cemetery because he was a Northerner?

I asked, "Are you here, Mr. Fendall Sutherland?"

A man answered: "Yes."

"What year did you die?"

"1833."

"Any Sutherlands alive during the War Between the States?"

A male voice said: "Madame?"

"My name is Pamela. What is yours?"

No answer.

"Mr. Sutherland?"

"No!"

I wandered over to a tombstone to the left of me. "Who is Missy Ella? Are you here?"

A woman replied: "Yes."

Emma asked if I was going to do her family's cemetery, so I let her lead me to the fenced-in area. She pushed the gate open, and I stepped inside. Early evening was fast approaching, and I saw the pinks and oranges that spoke of sunset's arrival. I asked if any of the Olgers were still hanging around.

One man said: "What's up?" I pressed for the year of death and more, but did not get a response.

On my way to the battlefield of Sutherland Station and my car, I paused by the kitchen, took some pictures, and did a short EVP session, but got nothing (as I learned when I listened the next day). I snapped more photos and walked around the house. Dropping off most of my equipment except the EMF meter, my one recorder, and ghost box, I did a quick ghost box session. During the whole time, the EMF meter displayed no readings.

"I heard that the house had been used as a Union hospital for the Battle of Sutherland Station here."

A man spoke: "Yes. Fork Inn."

"Did you leave a girlfriend or wife behind?"

Nothing.

"Did you leave parents behind?"

A younger male voice: "Yes."

"Are there any Confederates here right now?"

"Yes."

"Did they die here, too?"

"Fate."

I saw that it was 8:30 p.m. by then and the sky was growing darker, so I said, "Goodbye. I have to leave for home now. Please do not follow me home."

"Bye."

I said, "Thank you, and have a good night."

"You, too."

The next morning, I returned for my tablet that I'd left behind. Before I drove back home to escape what would be the soon-to-be 99° heat, I dropped by the Olgers Store Museum across the street from the Battle of Sutherland Station memorial. Jimmy Olgers, the man who had told other Dinwiddie tales after the ghost tour, sat on the front porch with his friends. I saw a sign hung on the front wall of the building that said: 1908-1988.

Jimmy invited me to check out the museum. Crammed full of various things from the bizarre to nostalgic and historic, I walked through five rooms.

There were large turtle shells, a golden statue of a Civil War officer, a bottle labeled "100 Proof Geritol XXX," and much, much more. It was a place as interesting as Jimmy Olger himself. I dropped a dollar in the donations container (to help keep the museum going) before I stepped out into the humid heat.

Jimmy kissed my hand and called me a lovely lady. He then told me an experience he had concerning Sutherland Tavern. Some of his friends and he were sitting on the porch of the museum one day when he thought he saw curtains move at a window in the house. He blinked and told his friends what he'd seen. They didn't believe him. It happened again. He led his friends over to the house and, since he had a key, he unlocked the door and entered. He knew no one was home at the time, so there should have been no reason for the curtains to move. The men searched the building until they came to what had been the bedroom of Darrell's great-grandparents. They found an imprint on the bed there when there was no cause for it.

Drive by Sutherland Tavern one early evening and glance up at the window on the second floor. Don't be surprised if you see a lovely, dark-haired lady in white. It's just one of the resident ghosts daydreaming away.

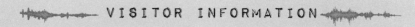

VISITOR INFORMATION

Sutherland Tavern
19621 Namozine Road
Sutherland, VA 23885

The Tavern is ten minutes west of Petersburg at the intersection of US Route 460 and Route 70 in Dinwiddie County. The Olgers have a website for Sutherland's Tavern Antiques at http://sutherlandstavernantiques.net.

Spooky Tales of Dinwiddie County

WHEN I SEE GHOSTS THEY LOOK PERFECTLY REAL AND
SOLID— LIKE A LIVING HUMAN BEING. THEY ARE NOT
MISTY; I CAN'T SEE THROUGH THEM; THEY DON'T WEAR
SHEETS OR BLOODY MUMMY BANDAGES. THEY DON'T HAVE
THEIR HEADS TUCKED UNDER THEIR ARMS. THEY JUST
LOOK LIKE ORDINARY PEOPLE. IN LIVING COLOR, AND
SOMETIMES IT IS HARD TO TELL WHO IS A GHOST.

—CHRIS WOODYARD

The Stolen Child

The Sutherland Tavern ghost tour in October 2013 included the old cooking kitchen where the slaves worked in 1834. Storyteller Jimmy Olgers sat in a chair by the fireplace and recounted a couple of Dinwiddie County's scary tales by the firelight in this room. Everyone sat or stood, crowding the room. I sat on a bench closest to the fireplace, and Bill leaned against the wall by the door. Jimmy told the following story.

Lou Joiner and her parents lived in a house on Trench Road long ago. Jimmy said the house was still there. Lou was six years old and outside playing with her doll and little dog. Maybe her mother looked away or went inside for a second. Back then, they didn't think of children being taken; but, suddenly, the little girl and the dog were no longer in the yard.

Her parents contacted the local law, and many people searched for the little girl. They discovered the doll lying on the bank of the creek, but they did not see one sign of the child. Her little dog came back four days later, shivering.

Someone mentioned that gypsies had been seen in the area. People thought that maybe one of the caravans had stolen her away.

Years later, in 1928, a woman stepped off a train that stopped at the depot. She walked over to a woman working there, and said, "I am Lou, the little girl who disappeared years ago from here."

The woman she spoke to had been the best friend of the child's mother and knew the little girl well back then. She said, "Come on home with me. I'll make supper for us, and you can tell me everything."

Both women talked into the night. The old woman leaned back, when all was said and done, to say, "You're no more Lou Joiner than I am Jesus Christ."

The young woman got back on the train and left Dinwiddie, never to return. Jimmy never explained why she came to the area to tell this story. He did say that the house had a curse on it. The fifteen-year-old son of one owner, Giles, was attacked by three dogs and killed. For thirty years, no one stayed in the house. Finally, some people moved in, and they're still living there.

Lou Joiner, though, was never found. Sometimes, it is said that screams are heard near the creek.

Haunted Group Home in Sutherland

This short story is about a woman who worked at a group home in Sutherland, on White Oak Road, for about six years. One day, she was left in the home by herself, as the other staff had taken the children out for an activity.

As she sat in the downstairs office, the house began to shake as if an earthquake was happening. She could actually see the vibrations on the walls. Sounds came from upstairs in the room above, too, like many people stomping on the floor with boots or moving around fast as if in a hurry to get somewhere.

This terrified her. She grabbed her purse, bolted from the place, and ran to her car, staying inside it until the others returned.

The guys who worked the overnight shift used to tell her that they'd heard screaming outside at night. Some of the children told the staff that the back door would slam shut by itself.

After six years at the job, she was glad when she left for another position.

Burnt Quarter

There is a legend about an old home: Burnt Quarter. It has an amiable ghost, who never harms anybody, though her ghostly presence may be felt. The legends claim that "Nissy" Coleman is the spirit that visits her bedroom on the second-floor east wing. On very still nights, it is said that you can hear the rustle of her skirts as she ascends the enclosed stairway, enters the room, and hovers about the bed. Servants decline to remain in the house alone after dark, though conceding that the spirit has never sought to harm them.

Burnt Quarter, or Gilliam's house, is a historic plantation. It was built in stages starting about 1750, and consists of a two-story, hipped roof, with a central section flanked by 1½-story wings. On April 1, 1865, the property became the scene of the Battle of Five Forks. During the battle, the house served both as headquarters for Union General Merritt and as a military hospital.

The plantation represented an example of descent through the female lineage, passing from the Colemans to the Goodwyns and ultimately to the Gilliam family. Much of the land where the Five Forks battle occurred was purchased from a descendant of the Civil War owner of Burnt Quarter. The house and surrounding farm lie south of the boundary of the park, although an easement has been granted to the National Park Service. The house represents the sole surviving dwelling dating prior to the Civil War in the immediate vicinity of Five Forks. It is claimed that family portraits slashed and damaged by Union cavalry during the Battle of Five Forks still hang on the walls of the house. It was listed in the National Register of Historic Places in 1969 and is privately owned.

COLONIAL HEIGHTS

CITIES, LIKE CATS, WILL REVEAL THEMSELVES AT NIGHT.

—RUPERT BROOKE

Colonial Heights, once a part of Chesterfield County, became a town in 1926, incorporated in 1948, and became an independent city in 1960. The name of Colonial Heights resulted from an incident during the American Revolutionary War. The French troops of Lafayette, in 1781, set up artillery on the heights overlooking the Appomattox River and Petersburg, where British forces were located.

There is a legend about an English soldier stationed in Petersburg. It is told that he saw Lafayette's troops across the river, and cried out, "Look! There are the Colonials, up on the Heights!" The name Colonial Heights was born. The name was given to a subdivision on the Oak Hill tract in 1906.

The earliest people to inhabit the area were members of the Algonquin Indian tribe who roamed along the Appomattox River. To this day, there are several areas in Colonial Heights that retain their Indian names.

British colonists settled the land in 1620, about two weeks prior to the settlement of Plymouth, Massachusetts. They sailed up the Appomattox River searching for clear land, and they finally settled in Conjurer's Field. This area was named by the Indians after one of their magicians (or also called conjurers or witches), who was thought to have cast spells over the confluences of the waters. Not long after, Charles Magnor registered the first land patent in the area for 650 acres. He developed this into a plantation before he sold it in 1634.

Brick House was built during the period 1677-1685 and is the oldest permanent structure in Colonial Heights. The house is owned by the Old Brick House Foundation. The first recorded settlement in Colonial Heights was owned by Thomas Shore who bought 144 acres in 1775, and built a mansion called Violet Bank. Violet Bank is now a museum owned by the city of Colonial Heights.

The city seal depicts the figures of the house and cucumber tree at Violet Bank. The flower commonly known as "Magnolia" is the floral emblem of the city. The city is located twenty miles south of Richmond, and is 120 miles south of the nation's capital. Petersburg lies directly across the Appomattox River. Colonial Heights is bordered to the south by Petersburg, to the east by the Appomattox River, and by Chesterfield County to the north. It has a land area of 8.15 square miles, or 5,216 acres and was once a part of Chesterfield County.

Colonial Heights also has Fort Clifton Park, a library, a Books A Million bookstore, schools, homes, businesses, an animal shelter, hotels, and Southpark Mall. Southpark has four department stores and eighty-five specialty shops. It is the premier shopping destination for the Tri-Cities area of Petersburg, Colonial Heights, and Hopewell, and home to a state-of-the-art movie theatre, Regal Cinemas Stadium 16, a food court, plus a Laser Force laser tag operation.

If you need to find anything out about Colonial Heights, such as locating restaurants, hotels, or a shop, you can find out more at www.colonialheightsva.gov/.

But if you need to learn more about its unseen residents, keep reading.

Violet Bank Museum

A HOUSE IS NEVER STILL IN DARKNESS TO THOSE WHO
LISTEN INTENTLY; THERE IS A WHISPERING IN DISTANT
CHAMBERS. AN UNEARTHLY HAND PRESSES THE SNIB OF
THE WINDOW, THE LATCH RISES. GHOSTS WERE CREATED
WHEN THE FIRST MAN WOKE IN THE NIGHT.

— J.M. BARRIE

Violet Bank House with the cucumber tree—creepy looking without its leaves.

Located at 303 Virginia Avenue, Violet Bank Museum is filled with much history and paranormal activity. Confederate General Robert E. Lee used Violet Bank Farm for his headquarters. He could see Petersburg from there while the siege happened.

Today, the building is a superb example of Federal design and American interior decorative arts, as it interprets the period from 1815 to 1873. The present building replaced the first one constructed by Thomas Shore. Destroyed by fire in 1810, the house was rebuilt by Shore's widow, Jane Grey, and her second husband, Henry Haxall. There is a display of Civil War-era artifacts: guns, furniture, glass, ceramics, textiles, accoutrements, books, swords, and other things. It has one of the most sophisticated and beautiful Adam-style ceiling moldings in the country. Violet Bank Museum is on the National Register of Historic Places and is considered a Virginia Historic Landmark. The cucumber tree on the property is one of the largest in the world and is very rare east of the Blue Ridge Mountains.

Days at the Museum

On a rainy Saturday, December 14, Bill and I headed to the museum to see what we could find within its walls. A large tree with no leaves lurched out of the rainy darkness like a scary apparition. Was that the cucumber tree? The porch of the house was decorated with Christmas figures and looked quite charming. A woman dressed in a Victorian gown greeted us, and we walked through a room where music was being played, and I even saw a kid dressed like Tiny Tim. Santa Claus sat in a chair across the front hall in another room.

Being more interested in the history part of the museum, Bill led me downstairs to where there were displays of weapons of all kinds and clothing from Civil War era. He asked a docent why the house was called Violet Bank, and the man told us that most homes in those days were named. The owner, liking violets, christened this one Violet Bank. Since photographs with flash weren't allowed inside the house, we just walked around, looking at the historical displays. Staying beneath my umbrella to keep my camera protected and dry, I shot some pictures outside before we left.

I returned on December 20, 2013, a nice sunny day, to talk to Russ Walburn about the history and paranormal happenings of the museum. I remembered being told that he was usually there Fridays, but I found that it was his week off when I got there. I asked the male docent who was there before I left if he'd had any experiences, paranormal-wise. He said, "Nothing I would admit to." In other words, he had, but he wouldn't tell. He was the only person in the building at the time.

I took some shots of the front and back of the house, the cucumber tree, and the yard. I did a short EVP session outside and turned on my EMF meter out back. For a quick second, a second light blinked, then went out. Were the ghosts of the place on duty?

When I got home, I uploaded the photos, enlarging them to check out the windows. The window to the far right at the back of the house had nothing in it. The second and third photos of the same window revealed what looked like a woman with her hair up, all in gray, peering out! I planned to ask Russ about it. Others saw the photos and told me the figure looked like a woman as well.

Close-up of the woman looking out the window taken in December 2013. There was no woman in the museum that day, just the one male docent alone in the house, who happened to be downstairs in the Civil War Museum.

Except for me, there was no one else outside on the street, in their yards, or on porches of the homes in the neighborhood.

I got two EVPs from the session that day. One was a woman's voice after I asked at the back of the house, "Can you tell me your name?" Like I said earlier, no one was outside of their homes, and no other vehicles drove down the street in back or out front. It was a weekday, so most people may have been at work. There had been no children playing outside either.

So, who was the woman at the window, and whose voice did I hear? Sadly, the voice was low pitched, so I couldn't get her identity.

The second EVP came after I asked, "Were you here when the War Between the States happened? When Lee used the parlor in the house for his quarters during the Siege of Petersburg?" Same feminine voice, but too low to catch what had been said.

I returned Friday, December 27, 2013 to take a tour of the house. Russ came to the front door to let me in for my tour. This included the Civil War museum downstairs in the basement and, after, upstairs in the house.

I got an email from him a week later with a date to conduct an investigation of the museum.

The Investigation

I revisited the museum on Sunday, January 12, 2014. No one was touring the museum or outside on the property. The neighborhood was quiet, and the only noise came from outside from chains on the front porch banging together. Russ let me in through the back entrance, and told me he would be doing some reading in his office downstairs. I took out one recorder and placed it in one room in the Civil War museum downstairs and let it run to see if I would catch anything. I decided to begin EVP and ghost box sessions in the room holding cannonballs and other items from the Civil War.

At home and listening to my recordings later, I caught what was unmistakably footsteps as I was doing the EVP session. Not *in* the room, but outside of it. These sounded close enough to be going between the two glass cases of weapons to the right of me when leaving the room. I listened to the other recorder first and thought the footsteps came from outside the room and might have been Russ. But the docent had stayed in his office and was reading. After I heard this recording, I listened again to the other recorder and realized those footsteps happened while I was in the other room—I heard my own voice faintly conducting the EVP session!

During the ghost box session, I asked at one point, "Can you give me your name?" I did this several times, until I received three names: "Drake." "Pike." "Greg."

"Are you attached to the weapons in the museum here?" I asked.

"Yes." Another voice blurted: "No."

"Did you have a girlfriend or a wife when alive?"

I thought I heard "Beatrice," but I cannot say that for sure.

I tromped upstairs to investigate the house itself. The boots I wore *clomp, clomp, clomped* up the steps in my recording. I put down my bag on the floor of the landing, took out a notebook and laid it on the floor, and tried my EMF meter for the first time. I found its batteries had died and, not having replacements, I began an EVP session to ask a number of questions.

"Tell me your name. How many spirits are with me? Women or men? Did you belong to the house when alive?"

At first, I got nothing. But as I listened later at home, I stilled myself and backed up the recording until I heard it the second time: a woman's voice speaking the same time as mine. Because of my voice being closer to the recorder, it was louder, so I couldn't catch what she said.

I decided to head to the hallway and, after that, the parlor, returning to the Short Room (where people from tours were taken), talking as I did.

As I almost stepped into the hallway, I heard the creak of a door. "I heard a door. Who was that?"

A man's voice could be heard from the recording: "It was Bridget." (It sounded like "Bridget," or something close to that.)

I demanded, "Can you make that door open or close again?" Nothing.

"Can you tell me your name?"

A woman's soft laugh issued from the recorder. Then *ping, pong,* like something dropping, I thought.

Now, all this time, I heard the banging of metal like chains that had come from outside, just like the last time. So I knew the sounds of things I heard live, besides catching them on the recording.

I heard a man begin talking and realized Russ was talking to someone on a phone downstairs. There had been no ringing, so he had called out. Eventually, his voice died off.

I asked, "Were you here when that cucumber tree was planted?"

Footsteps and a swishing like a woman's skirts could be heard. Suddenly, as I asked another question, I heard a woman's voice, "Hello?"

Hello to me? Or hello to another spirit?

When I returned with my bag slung over my shoulder and placed the recorder on a chair in the Short Room, I went to grab my notebook and discovered it lying face down, partly in the Short Room with its bottom half in the area with the stairs. It had traveled maybe twelve inches from where I'd left it near the steps going down.

Putting it away, I wandered into the Short Room and asked if anyone was with me. Deciding it was time to go back downstairs, I went to take my recorder off the chair when the hair on my right arm stood straight up. A bone-chilling cold covered my whole arm, slithering over to my side and then over all of me. I looked down to my right and dipped my hand to find a small circle of freezing air. Stepping away from that spot, I grew warmer. I quickly picked up my recorder and crossed over to the stairs. As I put a boot down on the first step, I could swear I heard a woman giggling with my own ears. I looked, but saw nothing, and continued downstairs.

Sitting down on the last step, I did a ghost box session.

"How many spirits are with me?" No answer.

"How many male ghosts?"

A man's voice replied: "Six."

"Any women?" Nothing.

I used my heat thermometer and asked whoever was there to drop the temperature. I got them to bring it down to 65. Putting it away, I resumed the quizzing.

"My name is Pamela. What is yours? What did you like to do when alive? What did you drink when alive? Water? Wine? Ale?"

Off my recording, I got a whistle. Nothing else.

I turned on my ghost box again to perform a session.

"Will you tell me your name?"

A man's voice: "I can't tell you."

I asked, "Why can't you tell me your name?"

Another voice: "Jack."

"If you want me to stop, let me know, and I will."

"Yes, Pamela." Same man's voice.

Shutting off the ghost box, I put it away. I clicked off the recorder and stored it in the bag's pocket. Getting up, I went to grab my other recorder, stopped it, and put it with the first one. I said goodbye to Russ and left the museum.

Next time you step outside the Violet Bank Museum after a visit, don't be surprised if you find someone staring at you from one of the windows and, if you wave at the figure, you will realize you can see through them. This is only one of the ghostly inhabitants.

VISITOR INFORMATION

Violet Bank Museum
303 Virginia Avenue
Colonial Heights, VA 23834
804-520-9395
www.colonialheightsva.gov/Facilities/Facility/Details/Violet-Bank-Museum-44

Admission to tour the museum is free, though donations will be accepted. The building is open Tuesday through Saturday from 10 a.m. to 5 p.m. and Sunday from 1 p.m. to 6 p.m., closed on Monday. Group tours are welcome.

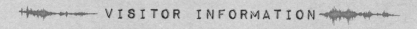

Old Brick House

GHOSTS CROWD THE YOUNG CHILD'S FRAGILE EGGSHELL
MIND.

— JIM MORRISON

The Old Brick House.

The Old Brick House was built in 1685 by Richard Kennon, an English gentleman. Considered the oldest brick house in the region, it is thought by some people to be the oldest in Virginia. The building is located on the promontory between Swift Creek and the Appomattox River and was called "Brick House." The peninsula where it stands is often referred to as "Conjuror's Neck," because an old Indian conjuror used to live there.

Besides history, there are legends of it being haunted by trapped Indian spirits. Could one of these phantoms be the Native Indian conjuror?

An Investigation

To see the outside of the house and do a paranormal investigation, I drove to Colonial Heights on March 28, 2014. The sky was painted with gray clouds and the sun struggled to peep through them. It lent an atmosphere to the empty house and surrounding quiet neighborhood. Parking the car on the street, I carried my camera around my neck and stuck my EMF meter, recorder, and ghost box in various pockets. It was 8:30 a.m. and the air felt cold and crisp. Though spring had come the week before, winter appeared to still have its claws in Virginia. Today's investigations would be done outdoors with plenty of footwork, so I wouldn't be sweating.

I started with an EVP session while I took some pictures and asked a few questions, hoping they would be answered.

"Is there anybody still haunting the land of this house or the house itself? What year is this? What year did you pass away? Do you have a name? First and last so I can verify it. Are you connected to the house?"

Later, I heard nothing on the recording at first. Most sounds were easy to explain, such as birds singing. Just before I got ready to turn on my ghost box, a feminine voice said: "Spirit world..." It sounded like that person had broadcast from far away.

The ghost box on, I went right into my questions. "Is there anyone here connected to the spirit world?"

A man said: "Yes."

"What is your name?" I got something—a partial: "Ken" or "Kennon"?

"Can you tell me what year you passed away?"

"Yes." Then whatever else the ghost said, static filled the airwaves.

I asked, "Do you know what year it is now?"

The man replied: "No."

"Are you connected to the house?"

"Yes."

"Can you tell me your name again?" Nothing.

I said, "My name is Pamela. Can you say my name back to me?"

No one said my name, so I pressed on, "Say Pamela, please."

A woman piped up: "Please..."

"My name is Pamela. That is all you have to say?"

"Nay."

I hoped the woman might answer my next question at least. "Are you connected to the Old Brick House?"

She said: "Brick house?"

"Are you connected or not? Yes or no?"

The man said: "No." Did he mean she wasn't? Earlier he had said he was. Or was this a different man?

"I heard there is an Indian conjuror attached to the land. Is he here?" I heard something, like three words, but they were indistinguishable.

"Anything you'd like me to tell the living for you?" No one replied to that.

I said goodbye and thank you, shut off the recorder and ghost box, and headed to my car. I drove away to my next destination of Fort Clifton Park in Colonial Heights.

Come visit the Old Brick House and its land. But know that it's not empty, not by a long shot. The inhabitants may not have left, even the Indian sorcerer could be around. He *may* still be practicing magic.

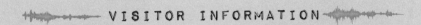

VISITOR INFORMATION

Old Brick House
131 Waterfront Drive
Colonial Heights, VA 23834

The property is owned and operated by the Old Brick House Foundation. If you wish to tour it, there is no admission fee for interior tours to the house or for exterior visits. Exterior views are open from dawn to dusk. For an interior tour, you will need to make an appointment by calling 804-520-9476.

Fort Clifton

LET US CROSS OVER THE RIVER AND REST UNDER THE
SHADE OF THE TREES.
—LAST WORDS OF THOMAS "STONEWALL" JACKSON

Front sign pointing out the park is Fort Clifton.

Fort Clifton was a Confederate stronghold on the Appomattox River, serving as an important link to the line that defended Richmond and Petersburg in 1864 and 1865. Located on a high bluff at the junction of the Appomattox River and Swift Creek, the fort controlled navigation on the river north of Petersburg and was a formidable defensive bastion that wasn't taken by Union forces until the fall of Petersburg on April 3, 1865.

Fort Clifton Park consists of twenty-four acres overlooking the Appomattox River. Earthworks crisscross the park as the site of Fort Clifton where five Union ships sailed to battle Confederate troops on June 11, 1864. The Confederate Battery, with cannon emplacements, remained in Confederate hands as the cannons drove the Union attackers away.

Right after I visited the exterior of Brick House, I set the GPS for Fort Clifton. But when it came upon the school to my left, the GPS's female voice stated: "You are here."

Here? The elementary school was to my left, while homes graced my right. I tried to remember where the park was, but it had been years since I'd been there. After turning around and coming back to the school, I saw the sign for the park showing it to be behind the school.

I parked my car in the parking lot. No one seemed to be using the area. I grabbed my ghost bag and wandered around the park after turning on my recorder, snapping a few pictures as I walked. I stopped at the section of the park that had the earthworks to begin an EVP session.

"Is anybody here? Any Civil War soldiers? Confederates? What year did the Union gunboats come upriver to fire upon you? Give me the date and year? Did anybody get hurt? Give me their names. Do you know what year it is today? Did you leave anyone behind? A girlfriend or a wife?"

As I listened later at home, I found I hadn't gotten any responses.

At the location, I switched on the ghost box.

I spoke over the scanning noise. "Any spirits with me? Say yes or no."

Nothing. I tried again. "What is your name?"

A man said: "Violet." Another, with a much deeper voice, joined in: "Worth."

"What is your rank, Worth?"

Another man came back with: "Speak?"

"Were you a Confederate soldier? Did you die here?"

Another man spoke up: "Fort." Was the ghost telling me it was a fort or he died here when it was a fort?

I said, "It is no longer a fort. This is a park now."

A male voice said: "Great."

I spat out the questions about the wife or girlfriend, her name, and if she was from Virginia. But one male voice just uttered: "City." At least that was all I received from that one, but another man chimed in: "....Carolina." Couldn't get if North or South as static flared up, vanishing with the Carolina part. Did he mean the woman's state or where *he* came from?

After I turned off the ghost box, I asked them to mimic a sound I made. I rapped on the sign. Immediately after, in the recording, I got lesser versions of my knocks!

I thanked them and said goodbye after explaining they could not follow me home. I left the park for Chesterfield.

The next time you take your kids to Fort Clifton Park for the day, don't be surprised if they tell you about the man in gray who tossed their ball back to them. It's just the Confederate soldiers still standing guard and waiting for the Union gunboats.

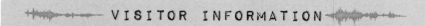 VISITOR INFORMATION

Fort Clifton Park
100 Brockwell Lane
Colonial Heights, VA 23834
804-520-9392
www.colonialheightsva.gov/Facilities/Facility/Details/Fort-Clifton-Park-34

Note: The park is behind Tussing Elementary School at 5501 Conduit Road in Colonial Heights.

The admission is free, and it is open year-round from seven in the morning to dusk. Each year on Mother's Day, the Fort Clifton Festival is held here. The festival is family-oriented and educational, portraying the historical significance of the fort. Arts and crafts are featured as well as Civil War relic exhibits and re-enactors. Children's rides, food concessions, and musical entertainment are also included.

PRINCE GEORGE'S COUNTY

HISTORY IS A MIGHTY DRAMOS, ENACTED UPON THE
THEATRE OF TIMES, WITH SUNS FOR LAMPS AND
ETERNITY FOR A BACKGROUND.

—THOMAS CARLYLE

Prince George County is south of Chesterfield County, and you can get there by traveling Route 10, or by going through it on Route 460 heading for Hampton Roads, or by exiting off 295 South. There is the Prince George Heritage Museum that contains pre-history to present day events of the area. Its artifacts and stories present the society and cultures of those who have settled and lived in Prince George, including the Native Americans, English settlers along the James River, African Indians, Czech-Slovaks, and others, too.

Prince George County was named for Prince George of Denmark, England's Queen Anne's consort. The county was formed from part of Charles City County. Before it became Prince George, the area was a corporation of the Virginia Company from May 1607 until 1613.

Monthly courts were held on the Charles City side from around 1623 until it became inconvenient for the settlers on the south side of the James River to make the water crossing. General Assembly in August of 1702 declared the lands on the south side of the river to be Prince George County. The county was officially established in July of 1703. Prince George is bordered on the north by Hopewell and the Appomattox and James Rivers, on the east by Surry County, on the south by Sussex County, and on the west by Petersburg and Dinwiddie County.

The only city in Prince George was Bermuda City (later City Point) in 1613. One of the original Jamestown survivors, John Martin, received a large land grant, Martin's Brandon in 1616. Benjamin Harrison built Brandon between 1765 and 1770, and it is the only National Historic Landmark in the county. Architectural evidence indicates that its design might be due to Thomas Jefferson. The towns of Petersburg and Blandford (established in 1748) were originally a part of the county. Blandford Church was built from 1735 to 1737 within what was called Bristol Parish. Later, Blandford became part of Petersburg.

During the Revolutionary War, Major General William Phillips led British forces through Prince George County where they attacked Americans defending Petersburg on April 25, 1781. The victorious British commander of this battle died in Petersburg on May 13. He is buried in the Blandford Church Cemetery in an unmarked grave that no one can find.

The Civil War figures much in Prince George's history. One of the county's native sons, Edmund Ruffin, is credited with firing the first shot of the war on April 12, 1861, at Fort Sumter. An agricultural innovator, he was born at Evergreen just east of present-day Hopewell. A rabid secessionist, Ruffin committed suicide after the end of the war in 1865.

Many Civil War earthworks were in Prince George County. From June

15-17, 1864, approximately forty percent of the Army of the Potomac crossed the James River on a 2,100-foot-long pontoon bridge from Weyanoke Point in Charles City County to Windmill Point at Flowerdew Hundred Plantation in Prince George County. Many battles occurred in the county during the siege of Petersburg. Battles like the one at Baylor's Farm (in present-day Hopewell) on June 15, Jerusalem Plank Road from June 21-24, Reams Station on August 25, and Confederate General Wade Hampton's Beefsteak Raid that occurred September 15-18. The most famous skirmish, Battle of the Crater, was fought in the county on July 30, 1864. Coal miners from the 48th Pennsylvania Volunteers dug a tunnel underneath the Confederate earthwork known as Elliott's Salient where they exploded 8,000 pounds of gunpowder.

Major historical developments in the county are the incorporation of Hopewell in 1916 and the virtual simultaneous establishment of Camp Lee. The new city of Hopewell contained historic City Point, as well as new chemical plants that had recently opened there. In June 1917, soon after American entry into World War I, Camp Lee was established on 8,900 acres of Prince George County. The camp became dormant when World War I ended. Survey work began on reopening the post for World War II in October 1940. When WWII ended, the camp was renamed Fort Lee.

The Department of the Interior and Department of Historic Resources created the Prince George County Courthouse Historic District on June 4, 2003. The district contains the 1883 courthouse and ten other buildings. The restored and renovated courthouse became the Prince George County Historical Museum on June 30, 2007.

One of the historical spots of the county is Merchant's Hope Church. It was placed on the National Historic Register on October 8, 1969. The name of Merchant's Hope comes from both a 1635 land grant on the James River and a barque (sailing vessel), *The Merchant's Hope*, both owned by transatlantic merchants in London. Richard Quiney, brother of the husband of Shakespeare's daughter, Judith, was one of those merchants. It is believed that, at a later time, Quiney actually owned the land.

Jerusalem Plank Road is also historical, as one of the first toll roads in America. It was known as Jerusalem Plant Road in 1853. It stretched from near Blandford Church all the way to Jerusalem (now known as Courtland in Southampton County). Plank roads were simply logs placed side by side. This was considered an early answer to the problem of getting stuck in the mud. Unfortunately, the life of such a road was short, as the planks deteriorated fast.

This is a county full of history. Is it also full of the supernatural? Read on to find out.

UFOs and Monsters

A UFO Fourth

A red ball of fire was spotted by four people on 295 South in the Prince George County area, around 10 p.m. on July 4, 2013. Could this have been leftovers from Fourth of July? Good question—but again, maybe not.

Goatman

THE SATYR WAS AT FIRST A MEMBER OF THE DISSOLUTE COMMUNITY ACKNOWLEDGING A LOOSE ALLEGIANCE WITH DIONYSIUS, BUT UNDERWENT MANY TRANSFORMATIONS AND IMPROVEMENTS. NOT INFREQUENTLY HE IS CONFOUNDED WITH THE FAUN, A LATER AND DECENTER CREATION OF THE ROMANS, WHO WAS LESS LIKE A MAN AND MORE LIKE A GOAT.

—AMBROSE BIERCE

It seems that a being with a hairy upper torso and the legs of a goat has been seen by teenagers in Prince George County. Six to seven feet tall, it makes one think of satyrs, or even Pan from Greek mythology. It always appears to teenage couples in secluded wooded areas at night. This "Goatman" rushes out from the trees and bangs its fists on cars, or through others' tales it is claimed the creature has a club or axe and it uses this on the vehicles. Frightened, the teenagers drive away. The proofs of the attacks are the marks on the metal.

The Goatman is explained by many different accounts. One concerns a government research facility near Washington, DC. An experiment went out of control and a scientist involved metamorphosed into a half-man, half-goat monster. He escaped to some nearby woods where, for years, he attacked couples parking in their cars at night. The problem with this explanation is that Prince George County is two- to two-and-a-half hours driving time away from DC. This same tale is also told in the Prince George's County located in Maryland. Here, in Virginia, another variation of the legend is told: there is an old hermit who lives in the woods and is seen walking alone at night along an unknown road. When anyone comes near him, he runs away. Still another legend has Goatman being a relative of the

New Orleans' evil chupacabra-like cryptid, the Grunch. Other terrifying legends spoken has the creature scouring neighborhoods, killing family pets, and breaking into people's houses to rape human victims.

Goatman has been reported in Alabama, Arkansas, California, Florida, Indiana, Louisiana, Kentucky, and Michigan. There was even one seen in Utah, until the creature proved to be nothing more than a man dressed in a goat suit, identified as a Southern California hunter preparing for an archery hunt of mountain goats.

This has all the makings of a good horror fiction story, mixing satyrs with a scary legend, but that's all it is: a story. The Goatman doesn't exist. Just tell yourself that over and over again, the next time you're in the woods alone in Prince George County in the dark of night and you hear a strange noise.

Sasquatch

Sasquatch, or Bigfoot as he has also been called, has been seen in Prince George County. If driving along the Route 10 portion of the county, with all the woods and country around you, there is the possibility of this furry ape-like being existing there with you. One sighting was reported on June 16, 2014, by *Cryptology News*. A man made a video about the occurrence and uploaded it to Youtube.

It was around six the night he saw it outside his yard. It stood at about fifteen feet. Both the man and the creature stared at each other, before the man went into his house and came back out, bearing a pack of Jack Links® for it. He tossed the package over the fence and reported that the bag wasn't there when he checked later. Now, I am not feeling confident about this, as the Jack Links® part of the story had me questioning his tale, considering Bigfoot is used in the product's commercials.

Another sighting happened back in 1979. A pregnant woman and her husband moved into a house on a road off Route 10 in Prince George. Their landlord lived 200 yards away. The first two months were quiet, but around December, when the woman's husband left for work, their dogs that lived outside (the landlord would not permit the dogs to be indoors), barked insanely until dawn broke. This kept up for a couple of months, until her mother came to stay with them after the birth of their baby. The first Monday the husband left for work, the barking began. This time, her mother heard it, too. When the young woman saw her little mixed terrier run toward something, snarling, then back away, she wondered what could be the cause.

Suddenly, she saw a long, hairy, black leg thrust out from around the corner of the house. When she ran to her mother, her mother said she saw someone out front. She said some car lights illuminated the figure, but she described it as someone tall and dressed totally in black. When the women contacted the police, they came to tell her the landlord claimed their daughter had an ex-boyfriend who had been harassing her and it was their opinion that it was him. She took the story, but wondered why the boyfriend would be bothering her place and not their's, since her husband and she had nothing to do with the landlord's daughter's problems.

At any rate, whatever stalked her home for weeks quit after the police checked out the woods and surrounding area. She always wondered if it could have been a Bigfoot, or if her mother was right, and it was a couple of them. Her husband wanted her and the baby away from there, so they moved away.

Ghost Bride of Brandon Plantation

WAS THIS LOVE? IT WAS LIKE A CONSUMING FLAME,
LICKING THROUGH MY DEFENSES AT A SLOW BURN.

— YANGSZE CHOO

Some ghost stories have to do with love, but this one involves unrequited love and vengeance. The haunted building involved with this tragic tale is Brandon Plantation in Prince George County. On what should have been the happiest day of her life, a young bride was the victim of unspeakable evil.

Jane Evelyn Harrison lived during the 1700s. She was just eighteen years old, and as the story goes, a ravishing beauty. Well aware of her beauty and not above using it along with her family's influence, she broke the heart of any man who fancied her. One such young man was Pierre Bondurant, a Frenchman, who fell for her hard.

They met at a spring dance, and after a short courtship, the Frenchman proposed marriage to Jane almost on a daily basis. Jane used every trick in the book to keep stringing him along. Just as he was about to embark on a long trip back to France, he asked for her hand again. Jane told him she would only marry him if her father agreed to the union. This young man was overjoyed as he left on his trip, but Jane knew her father would never agree to the match.

Jane was right. A month later, while in Paris, Pierre received a letter. It destroyed him. Jane had gotten engaged to another man and would be wed at Brandon Plantation in the fall. The worse then happened when Pierre was invited to her wedding.

Pierre mingled among over 100 guests gathering that November to see Jane Harrison marry Ralph Cocke. He approached the groom and asked if he might toast the couple first. His request was granted. Pierre raised his glass and said, "Whatever fate may be, and this day alone will tell, may both of you be happy and free from sorrow, malice, and ill." The wedding happened without incident, with a huge reception afterward.

During the party, Pierre drew Jane aside and offered her a glass of champagne. "Let us toast to our health," he said. Happy that he did not display any animosity towards her, Jane took the glass and drank it down. He told her he loved her when they first met and still loved her.

Pierre noticed that Jane's new husband heard what he had said, so he tossed back his own champagne, and left the house.

By the time the last guest left the party, Jane collapsed in the drawing room. She lay on her deathbed poisoned from the drink given to her by Pierre and she died that evening. As they prepared the body for burial, it was discovered that her wedding ring was missing. It turned up in the coat pocket of Pierre Bondurant, who was later found dead in the carriage that carried him from Brandon Plantation. The ring was returned to Jane's family, but her aunt who owned Brandon at the time, claimed the ring was cursed. She embedded the ring in the plaster of the ceiling over the spot where Jane fell.

Since that time, people working and living at Brandon began to see a ghostly image of a woman in white who appeared only in late November. Eventually, a woman named Helen bought the house. Helen was walking by the family cemetery on the grounds one night when she saw a figure drifting towards the house. She hurried back indoors and once safely inside, she heard a crash coming from the drawing room. She ran to investigate and found the same figure hovering over the floor. The figure appeared to be going from place to place before settling over a fallen piece of plaster. The ghost seemed to be looking for something. It looked up, then floated through the wall and vanished.

Helen dug through the fallen plaster and found a tarnished wedding ring. Figuring that's what the ghost was looking for, she had the ring suspended from the ceiling on a string. It remains there to this day, as does the ghost of Jane, still looking for her ring.

History

This home was designed by Thomas Jefferson, and is declared the first brick plantation house built in Virginia. It hit the auction block on June 26, 2013, only the third time it has changed hands since the colonization of Jamestown in 1607. The 4,487-acre property includes a seven-bed, 6.5-bath Palladian-style main house. The fields at Brandon, the "oldest continuous agricultural operation in the US," had continued to produce corn, wheat, and soybeans. The property also includes six square formal gardens, a swimming pool, tennis courts, and two river cottages. Nathaniel Brandon built the place around 1765 for his son, Benjamin. The home stayed in the Harrison family until 1926, when it was purchased by Robert W. Daniel, an RMS *Titanic* survivor. Daniel's son, a former US representative from Virginia, oversaw the operations of the working plantation until his death in early 2012. It is on the National Register of Historic Places in 1969, and further declared a US National Historic Landmark in 1985.

Originally, the acres were patented to John Martin in 1616. The tract was named Brandon after Martin's wife's family name. Martin was one of the original adventurers that accompanied Christopher Newport and served the Jamestown colony as a member of the First Council. Jamestown is located a few miles downstream from Brandon. In 1635, the property was sold to Richard Quiney

(Richard Quiney's brother Thomas was married to William Shakespeare's daughter Judith). The property was farmed by Quiney and his family until 1720, when it was sold to Nathaniel Harrison. At the death of Colonel Benjamin Harrison, the property was divided between his two sons and Upper Brandon plantation was created. Brandon remained in the Harrison family until acquired by Mr. and Mrs. Robert W. Daniel Sr. At that time, the Daniels undertook the restoration of the house and grounds.

The owners of Brandon had a history of public service. In addition to the Martin service in Jamestown, the Harrisons were a prominent political family in US history, producing numerous governors of Virginia and two US presidents. The Harrisons are also related to James Madison, Thomas Jefferson, George Washington, Ulysses S. Grant, and Winston Churchill. Mr. Daniel Sr. was a Virginia state senator and financier, besides a survivor of the sinking of the *Titanic*. His predecessors included an associate justice of the US Supreme Court, first attorney general of the US, and Secretary of State.

The *Progress-Index* mentioned that the house has been sold to a Florida company based out of Miami, Tiger Hill Holdings IX LLC. What that means for the house, I am not sure at this time.

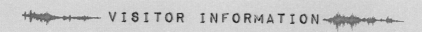

V I S I T O R   I N F O R M A T I O N

Brandon Plantation
23500 Brandon Road
Burrowsville, VA 23881
757-866-8486

North side of Brandon Road (five and a half miles north of Route 10, between Hopewell and Smithfield, in Spring Grove)

Gardens and grounds are open daily. There is an admission fee.

HOPEWELL

I NEVER FELT SALVATION IN NATURE. I LOVE
CITIES ABOVE ALL.

—MICHELANGELO

Hopewell was named after an English ship. Since its founding, the city has continued their British ties by twinning with the city of Ashford in Kent, England. Today, Hopewell consists of eleven square miles and is located at the confluence of the Appomattox and James Rivers. There is a marina at 1051 Riverside Road, along with various parks and playgrounds, a lovely library, schools, businesses, homes, historical attractions, and more.

Hopewell's City Point, the oldest part of the town, was founded by Sir Thomas Dale in 1613. This is the same man who also established Henricus. City Point was a small village when a Revolutionary War skirmish was fought on its banks. General Ulysses S. Grant directed the ten-month Siege of Petersburg from the grounds of Appomattox Plantation from 1864-1865. This historic home is now part of the City Point Unit of Petersburg National Battlefield.

Other pieces of the history of Hopewell include tobacco warehouses at City Point in the 1700s. A part of Benedict Arnold's expedition of British troops passed through City Point in 1781. It became a port of entry with a US Customs office in the early 1800s. Its post office moved from Bermuda Hundred, across the river, to City Point. The town of City Point was incorporated in 1826. The City Point Railroad Company was formed and runs between the city and Petersburg. Considered the oldest portion of the Norfolk and Western Railway, it is now a part of Norfolk Southern. It was one of the nation's earliest lines.

Union naval officers were ambushed after coming ashore to give medical aid to civilians in 1864, and there was a small skirmish with Confederate soldiers. General Butler's Army of the James occupied the area, and General Ulysses S. Grant set up his headquarters at Appomattox Manor in 1864. City Point became one of the busiest seaports in the world when the Union made its siege on Petersburg. The Union army also set up a hospital that was able to hold 6,000 people. Abraham Lincoln made presidential visits in 1864 and 1865.

City Point became a town again with 300 residents in 1870. By 1910, the same number still lived in City Point. Attracted by the seaport and rail facilities, the E.I. DuPont de Nemours Company purchased 800 acres at nearby Hopewell Farms in 1912, as they hoped to build a dynamite plant. DuPont also acquired 1,600 acres of the Eppes estate in 1914 to build the largest guncotton plant in the world during World War I. DuPont left at the end of the war; however, other manufacturing businesses took over, including Honeywell, Evonik Industries, Smurfit-Stone, and Hercules.

A fire decimated many buildings in 1915. The City of Hopewell was incorporated in 1916.

Hopewell is twenty-four miles southeast of Richmond, 132 miles south of Washington, DC, and the Port of Hampton Roads is seventy-five miles to the southeast. It is accessible by both I-295 and I-95, plus Route 10.

Historical attractions in Hopewell include: Weston Plantation, the City Point Open Air Museum, City Point Early History Museum at St. Denis Chapel, and Grant's Headquarters at City Point. Another interesting place is the Beacon Theatre at 401 North Main Street. Originally named the Broadway Theatre, it was built in 1928. A three-story vaudeville and movie theater with storefront commercial space, it also had second-floor apartments and third-floor meeting space. Listed in the National Register of Historical Places in 2000, the Beacon Theatre remained a theater offering live performances and movies until it closed in 1981. Renovated, the Beacon Theatre 640-seat auditorium reopened and hosted its first major event on January 13, 2014, with Leon Russell.

There are also eight mail-order homes from the Sears Catalogue built from 1926-1937. You can view these by driving through the Crescent Hills neighborhood. Stop by the Hopewell Office of Tourism and Visitor Center at 4100 Oaklawn Boulevard, to get a brochure on the homes. It is open Wednesday–Saturday, 9 a.m.–5 p.m. and Sunday, noon–4 p.m., and closed on major holidays.

Hopewell is a bustling city of the living. But even more so, the dead still reside there. Read on to see what I mean.

The lit historical Beacon Theater on 401 N. Main Street, in Hopewell, makes a charming sight in the early evening.

Weird Tales of Hopewell

I'VE ALWAYS DREAMED OF HAVING A YEAR-ROUND HAUNTED HOUSE.

—ELI ROTH

Haunted Sears Catalogue House

As I noted in the chapter about the city of Hopewell, there are eight mail-order homes from the Sears Catalogue that were built from 1926-1937. You can see these places today in the Crescent Hills neighborhood. A lady working at the Hopewell Office of Tourism and Visitor Center in May 2014 told me that one of the Sears Catalogue homes is supposed to be haunted due to a murder. She wasn't sure which home it was, though.

Indian on Horseback

There is a story about a person whose vehicle broke down on Route 10 in Hopewell, very close to the bridge. The person noticed a black horse with an Indian warrior walking beside it. As they drew closer, the person saw that neither the horse nor the warrior had a face. The Indian gave a war whoop, then both he and the horse disappeared.

UFOs Over Hopewell

A triangle-shaped UFO had been spotted in Hopewell on December 16, 2011, around six o'clock in the evening. On January 19, 2012, someone reported hearing strange sounds coming from the sky from 11 p.m. to midnight in Hopewell. Last, but not least, a triangle-shaped UFO was seen hovering over Hopewell on February 17, 2014, for ten minutes.

Weston Plantation House

GHOSTS, LIKE LADIES, NEVER SPEAK TILL SPOKE TO.
—RICHARD HARRIS BARNHAM

Weston Plantation House.

Most of the time when someone sees a ghostly form of a man or woman, it is white or gray. There are those instances where the spirit can also appear in color, such as the Lady in Red at Wrexham Hall in Chesterfield or the lady in blue at Weston Plantation House in the city of Hopewell.

The last time I'd been to the plantation house was when I was conducting research for *Haunted Richmond II* in 2011. My GPS had many issues finding the address. Weston's phantoms were working against me. I finally got proper directions and arrived at the house in the afternoon. Two cars were parked in the driveway, both belonging to people who worked at the plantation, including a tour guide and the woman working in the gift shop.

Weston sits on about one acre of land that is left from the vast amount the plantation once possessed. Homes, a street, a cemetery, and apartments jostled for space on land sold from most of the estate.

Weston Manor was built in 1789 by the Gilliam family. Listed on the National Register of Historic Places, this home retains eighty-five percent of the original woodwork. Its distinctive moldings, wainscoting, and chair rails are described as a classic example of Virginia Georgian architecture. They did not include the furniture, as the Dolans, who owned it up to the 1920s, took a lot with them when they left.

The Gilliams arrived in Virginia during the seventeenth century as indentured servants. By the late eighteenth century, the family had amassed several plantations in the area. William Gilliam's wife, Christian, was the daughter of Richard and Christian Robertson Eppes of nearby Appomattox Plantation. Her grandfather on her mother's side was a descendant of Pocahontas.

The Gilliams owned slaves, but the Historic Hopewell Foundation wasn't sure how many, just that it wasn't as many as other plantations had.

When the Gilliams passed away, others took possession of the plantation. Mainly, it was mariners and there was a good reason for this. One side of the plantation faces the Appomattox River and ships could stop by with visitors and things needed by the family living there. Being a working plantation, crops could be taken to market by boat, which was much faster than by horse and wagon.

During the War Between the States, the house became caught in the crossfire between the North and South as they battled. A cannonball landed above the ceiling, and one hundred years later, it crashed through the ceiling to the first floor.

A twelve-year-old girl, Emma Wood Richardson, fled with her family from Hampton, Virginia, when the North occupied it. Her father, being a river pilot, guided the family up river until they came to Weston. They stopped and stayed there for a short time from 1863 to 1864. Though her family had hoped to escape the war, it appeared they'd landed in the thick of things instead.

She wrote about her time in a diary, and called Weston, "Western." Years later, her diary was published, and I bought a copy from the Historic Hopewell Foundation's All Manor of Things gift shop in the reconstructed laundry dependency. (The laundry and the summer kitchen dependencies are both replicas. None of the other buildings, other than Weston, had survived when the Foundation took over.) Later, during the war, the house was used as headquarters by Union General Philip Sheridan.

The last family to farm the plantation was the Dolan family. They lived in the house until 1922, and then it went downhill. In 1962, the Broyhills acquired it. In 1971, it was transferred to the Historic Hopewell Foundation and opened to the public for tours in 1988.

The first thing I did after entering through the basement door was to watch a film about the house. The basement housed the winter kitchen. Besides the room where I watched the film, there was a modern kitchen through one doorway and two restrooms. Afterwards, the tour guide showed me the basement and pointed out the beams that rose up into the house, but they were well hidden in the walls. She pointed out the dumbwaiter that brought food up to the dining room above and believed it might have been there since the Gilliams, as Christian was related to Thomas Jefferson, who had a dumbwaiter at Monticello. However, she wasn't sure when Jefferson had built his own dumbwaiter.

After the tour was completed, the tour guide told me about the lady in blue. At that point, the bell on the door knob outside rang. She answered the door to tell whoever stood on the porch to go around to the basement door and wait. Instead, she just stood there, staring out. I went to peer out the window and only saw three vehicles; hers, mine, and the one belonging to the gift shop employee. She closed the door as she came back in, looking dumbfounded.

"Must have been a breeze," she said. The funny thing was when I left to go home, I felt no breeze at all. Was the lady in blue letting us know she was there or maybe she didn't like being talked about?

I heard about some other ghostly phenomena on May 9th, plus read about others later. One man at the house mentioned that sometimes the alarm would go off at 2 a.m. for no reason at all.

Another man who was part of the foundation, Charles Traina, talked to me in the gift shop and told me he usually used the bathroom in the house as there were none in the gift shop. He left the gift shop and headed for the front door (he had keys to get in).

Meanwhile, inside the building, the tour guide was in the office when she heard the front door open and slam shut. She peeked out, but there was no one besides herself in the house. A glance out her window revealed her co-worker crossing the lawn. Who made the noise? The front door was always kept locked—one needed a key to enter. Those who toured the house always went to the side entrance to the basement.

When Charles stepped indoors, she told him about her experience. "I thought it was you coming through the front door, but then I saw you coming from the gift shop."

She had heard about the strange phenomena in the house, such as footsteps across the floors, but had never experienced them herself, until that moment.

A former Weston Plantation tour guide talked about seeing a floating feminine spirit in the historic house. Though the guide could not discern any face, the hair appeared wavy and flowing, and when the ghost dissipated, it disappeared from the bottom up. The tour guide believed the spirit did not like her and that maybe the ghost was acting out on purpose. She also arrived at the house around the Fourth of July and from the floor in the parlor, it smelled like something had died there.

Ghost book author L. B. Taylor mentioned that a baby has been heard crying in the home. Stories of children heard playing and apparitions seen on the second floor have been told. Some investigators captured what sounded like a baby crying, but they determined it mechanical and nothing more. There are reports about a door that keeps swinging open. Someone decided to remove it from its hinges and reverse it. The swinging stopped. The odor of cigar smoke has been smelled in the front parlor. A tour guide heard phantoms cleaning a fireplace.

Outdoor EVP/Ghost Box Session
MAY 9, 2014

I did a quick EVP and ghost box session in the back of the house which faced the Appomattox River. The only thing the EVP recorded was a short burst of feminine voices; however, I caught a few more things with the ghost box.

I asked, "Anyone here connected to the house?"

A man replied: "Yes."

"What is your name?"

"Bart."

"Is there a woman connected to the house here?"

Male: "Yes."

"Can you let her speak?" No answer.

"Can you give me a name—first and last?"

Another male voice. "Philip," then something unidentifiable.

"Are you part of the Civil War? The War Between the States?"

"Yes." When I was able to look up some of the history I had for the house, I saw that Union General Philip Sheridan had occupied the house. Was this Philip connected to the Civil War?

I posed another question, "Is there a servant or slave to do with the house here?"

Another male voice spoke up: "Yes."

"Your name?"

"Bishop." It sounded like Bishop.

"Who did you work for that owned the house? Name?"

"... ... ... Gil...am." Gilliam?

I pressed for the name again, but my box went to straight radio. Had someone switched it off?

"Did you turn off the ghost box?"

A female voice popped up: "No." Could this be the mysterious lady in blue seen at Weston?

"Is this the lady in blue? I mean, the lady who has been seen dressed in a blue gown?" No answer.

I tried again to get an answer from her. "What is your name?"

"C........" This was all I could understand, as static covered up the rest of the name or what was being said.

"Thank you, if you gave me your name, can you say it to me again, as I didn't get that." Just scanning radio waves.

"Well, I have to go. Thank you for your answers, and I hope to return. Goodbye."

"Goodbye...." A couple of voices said this.

I made a call to Jessica about being able to do an investigation inside the house. She agreed. There was a tour guide on Sunday who had been at a paranormal investigation at the house some time ago. I could interview her about that investigation and what they found in their research, as well.

A New Interview

I drove back to Weston on Sunday, May 18, 2014, arriving at 12:40 p.m. Everything was set for 1 p.m. A couple of vehicles had parked closer to the house, and I discovered two families out on the docks as I wandered into the backyard. A large canopy was set up on the right side of the house for the concert held at 4 p.m. Finally, the tour guide drove up and parked beside my car.

Her name was Erin Winn. She unlocked the front door, and we entered the doorway, passed the staircase, a closed small door, and went into the office.

We began with the interview first. I asked if anyone else had experienced any of the ghosts here. She told me her French teacher, who was also a ghost tour guide in Richmond, had climbed up the stairs and thought it had grown colder as she did. People always stated feeling tired after being in the house, as though something was zapping their energy. One little girl, who toured with her mother, told Erin she was being rude to the lady she'd left downstairs. When her mother asked, "What lady?" The girl replied, "The dress-up lady." That scared the mother, especially since none of the tour guides wore costumes.

Erin took some paranormal investigators on a tour one night in December 2013. They had broken up into three groups. Erin took her group outside into the backyard. While they were out there, it felt as though a lot of people were watching them from the house. When they got to the docks, a female investigator remarked, "Who is the lady that passed by the windows indoors?" These windows looked into the dining room where the lady in blue has been seen passing by them by others in the past. And though very quick, the investigator felt certain the woman she saw wore something blue.

Erin told me that Union General Philip Sheridan's ghost has been seen walking from the woods to the back porch of the house. (The investigators hoped to catch him that night.) The funny thing was, a "Philip" was in my EVPs from May 9th, which were taken at the very spot where he always stopped!

Other phenomenon happened that night when everyone gathered inside the trailer that was parked out front; footsteps could be heard walking in the gravel around it. When they looked, they found nobody and saw nothing. When one of the investigators stepped out to smoke, she stated she could hear something walking in the gravel, but saw nothing. Upstairs, one of the investigators did the "shave and a haircut" knocking routine on the wall. He received two squeals on his EMF meter, so obviously it was a modern spirit. They also discovered that Sheridan did not want Erin reading his Bible that was kept in the Guestroom. One investigator's hair stood up as if a small childish hand mussed it. They also played a game with dowsing rods in the basement by hiding specific items and having the entities find them by pointing to the spots. Two out of five items were located.

My Investigation

First-Floor Hallway

Erin and I began my investigation when we walked out into the first-floor hallway. The grandfather clock clicked away, chiming on the hour. Otherwise, the building was quiet. I began an EVP session hoping to capture one word or a sound. When I listened later at home, I heard nothing except our voices, creaks from our feet, and the *click, click, click* of the clock.

I turned on my ghost box switching it to AM from FM, then the box went from radio to its scanning mode.

I asked, "Is there anyone here of the spirit world?"

A woman's voice answered, low and soft: "Yes."

"Is that a yes?"

The woman spoke louder this time: "Yes!"

I swept a glance around the place. "Is Philip here? The Philip I talked to last Friday?"

A man spoke: "Yes."

Another man, with a deeper voice said: "Philip." Two different male voices. Which one was Philip?

"Union General Philip Sheridan?"

The man with the deeper voice said something, but the clock chimed at that exact moment, so I couldn't tell what he said.

I pressed on. "Is the lady dressed in blue here? Can she speak?"

The woman from earlier didn't answer. I'd hoped it was her, but the lady from Friday didn't talk much, either.

"I would love to see your pretty dress."

The woman piped up: "You can't see it." I wondered if it was because she wouldn't allow me to see it or due to her being invisible?

"Anyone else here? Is there a Bart or Bishop here? The two males from Friday?" A couple of words were mumbled; however, they were too low to tell what was being said.

I asked the lady again, "To the lady, can you speak?"

"No."

"Why? Let me know the reason, and I will accept it."

A male voice blurted: "Why?"

Another male voice broke in and said some words that I couldn't quite catch. I shut off the ghost box as we gathered the equipment and walked past the grandfather clock into Mr. Gilliam's office.

Mr. Gilliam's Office

Erin led me into what had been Mr. Gilliam's office until he passed away, and then Mrs. Gilliam took it over for a while. I asked Erin if anything had happened in here. She stated she didn't know of anything specific. It was a lovely room with hardcover books in glass bookcases and antique furniture from the time frame it represented.

I tried a session, but no one said anything.

The Dining Room

As we entered the dining room, Erin told me that the lady in blue had been seen in the backyard passing by the two windows in the room. I tried my recorder in here.

"Is Philip Sheridan here? How about Bishop?" I figured Bishop as a servant might have served the family at the table.

"Is Mrs. Gilliam with us? I understand it's your home and we are your guests." I begin to suspect that maybe the mysterious lady in blue might be Mrs. Gilliam herself. I had no real proof unless she said it to me, though.

As I listened to the recording I'd made later, I heard a woman say: "Shut the door!" I wasn't sure what she meant by that. Was it an intelligent haunt, or maybe a sentence from the past?

The doorbell rang, and Erin went to answer the front door. I was left alone.

"Are you here with us right now?" I took a few steps. "You don't have to stay here, you know. You can go beyond the veil. The Foundation is taking good care of the house. Don't you agree?"

Just then, a thick cloud of oppression overcame me along with a creeping coldness. Was Mrs. Gilliam upset with me? When Erin came back, she stated she felt it, too. We stepped into the hallway, and the oppressed sensation dissipated.

Upstairs Hallway

We climbed the stairs to the second floor and stopped at the bedroom on the far right at the front of the house. Erin explained this was the children's room. I did a short EVP session asking if Emma was there. I heard nothing on the recording relating to this. I pulled out my ball that lit up in red and green colors if hit or bounced. I placed it on the floor and asked if she would like to play with it, and if she enjoyed playing ball with her friends. I received no answer and saw no movement of the ball. We left it there, just in case.

When I turned on the ghost box, I achieved results.

"Is Emma here?"

A young girl answered: "Yes."

"Emma?"

Again, she said: "Yes."

I hadn't really heard the two positive responses as she had spoken in a soft voice. I heard it over my headphones at home.

"Who is here? Is anybody going to talk?"

The girl spoke again: "I did!"

I heard her that time.

A male voice chimed in: "I'm sorry..."

"Who said 'I'm sorry...'?" No one replied to my question.

"Philip Sheridan? Are you with us?" Nothing.

"What about Bart? Who's Bart? Bishop? Who is Bishop?"

A man spoke up: "Philip. Sheridan."

I nodded. "Ah, Philip."

I said, "Erin, let's try another bedroom."

She agreed and led me down the hall to the bedroom on the same side as the children's. This room's windows looked out into the back yard where people were gathering and the musicians were getting out their instruments.

The Guest Bedroom

Erin stated that during the investigation in December, they'd thought someone had been sitting on the bed in the guest bedroom. They had found a dent in the bedspread.

I performed an EVP session first.

"Whose bedroom was this, once upon a time?"

A man replied: "Mine."

I asked a few more questions, then employed the ghost box.

"Philip, is this the bedroom you used when you were here?"

A male voice said: "Yes."

Another male voice spoke up. "Bart here."

"Who is Bart?"

"Me."

Okay, now I had a smart-aleck phantom. "Are you related to any of the people in this house, Bart? Or did you work for Philip Sheridan? Are you a Civil War soldier? What year did you die?"

The other male voice spoke: "Sheridan."

Was he telling me that Sheridan was still here, or that Bart had something to do with him? I wasn't sure.

Erin picked up the Bible on the table and told me that at the last investigation she had been told Sheridan didn't like her reading from it.

I nodded and said, "Is this Philip Sheridan's Bible? Why is Erin not allowed to read it?"

The same man called Philip said: "Belongs to me."

If he said he owned the Bible, that meant he must be Sheridan.

"Can she read from it now?"

"No."

I switched off the ghost box and just used the digital recorder. "Can you sit on the bed? Make some kind of movement?" I took my pendulum out of my pocket. "Is this Philip? If it is Philip, make the purple stone at the end of the chain move in a circle." The pendulum did not move.

"Is Bart here? If you are, then the same thing for you. Make it go in a circle if you are here. I cannot do it, you must do it as if you are taking your hand and holding the stone."

The pendulum barely moved at first, but soon, it spun faster and faster in a clock-wise circle. If we were not being fooled, Bart was with us. I asked him to stop, and the stone ended its momentum.

Erin suggested we do like another investigator did back in December and properly introduce ourselves. She stuck out her hand as if she was going to shake someone's hand, said her name was Erin, and she was pleased to meet him. I did the same with my pendulum dangling from my fingers and said, "Pleased to meet you." Something cold touched my hand, then it left. Had I felt something? Erin said something had pressed against her hand.

I slipped the pendulum back into my pocket. "Can you bring up the other lights on my EMF meter? I cannot." I waved my hand in front of the meter to show the spirits. "See? Nothing happened. But you can make the second light and the rest come on." I stepped back. During the whole investigation, I grew disappointed that nothing happened with the meter. "How about making something move for us? Verify you're here. Can you blow those tassels on the canopy?"

We stared at the tassels.

Erin said, pointing, "I see one moving."

I turned my head where she pointed and saw one of the tassels moving slightly. "I see it."

Erin noticed another.

I asked, "Can you move one more?" A third one swung back and forth.

I heard a sound of something scraping outside the bedroom. I thought it could be someone who had entered the house and was coming upstairs, but no one came to the bedroom.

I asked, "Did you hear that?"

Erin hadn't.

"Let's head for the chamber across the hall." Erin agreed and we grabbed all our equipment. As we exited the room, I looked back and said, "Come on, Bart or whoever else, join us in the next room."

The Master Bedroom

Erin mentioned that we were now in the master bedroom. From the Gilliams and down to the Dolans, all the owners had slept in this room. I brought out my green laser grid pointer and pressed the button. Green dots filled the hallway outside the bedroom. After a couple of seconds being on, I saw a flash of a white wispy thing about the height of a tall person pass through the green dots, head down the hallway toward the stairs, and then vanish. Had that been the top of some ghost not fully formed? It was nothing provable, but it was still exciting to have a personal experience like that. I wished it had been a solid visage though.

I pulled my dowsing rods from my bag and held them in front of me.

"Is anyone here? Cross the rods if you are able."

The rods crossed.

"Can you open them, please?"

They opened.

"Is this Bart? Cross the rods if that is so."

The rods didn't move.

"Is it Sheridan? Cross the rods if you are here."

They did not cross.

"Is the lady in blue here? Mrs. Gilliam?"

The rods crossed for me. Did Mrs. Gilliam finally admit to being the lady in blue people have seen?

"Can you uncross them for me?" They did. "Thank you."

"Is Emma Richardson here? Did you like the ball I brought? Would you like to play again with your friends? Please let us know you are here."

The rods intersected.

"Open them for me, pretty please."

The rods swung apart.

I handed the rods over to Erin and let her try them.

Erin said, "Emma, want to cross the rods for me?"

They did not move.

I said, "You can't? Yes, you can. Play the game, Emma."

Erin asked, "Are you too tired, Emma?"

I inquired, "Or do you want to go out and play?" I looked out the window where more people sat on the lawn, including some children playing. "I see some kids. Cross the rods if you see the kids outside."

Erin said, "Just cross the rods, and we will let you go out and play. Come on, you can do it." She flashed me a look and said, "I can feel the rods shifting."

Music from a guitar boomed from outside as the musicians warmed up for the upcoming concert.

I said, "There's music out there. You can go hear the music if you cross the rods."

The rods crossed over.

I nodded. "Go outside and play. But open the rods up first."

The rods separated.

"Thank you, very, very much"

Erin said, "Is Bart here? Crossing means yes, keeping them open means no."

Since my recorder was on, I asked, "Can you tell me your last name? Are you connected to the house? Were you a Civil War soldier?" When I listened later, I heard nothing at this part of the recording.

We put away the rods, and I swapped it for the ghost box. The scanning radio waves filled the room.

"Bart, are you with us in this room? Yes or no? Please say, yes or no."

"Yes."

"Last name? What is your last name?"

He said something, but it was too low and garbled within the scanning.

Erin touched her skin above her blouse and admitted to being touched there twice.

I said with a stern voice, "We do not touch any lady here."

The man's voice asked: "But why?"

"Why? You know why..."

He didn't say anything.

I gave my last name, hoping to make him share his own. A last name could be useful in finding out more about Bart. "My last name is Kinney, so what is yours?

He said something. "Ell... or Hel..." The rest of what he said was garbled.

I wanted to be sure Emma was still not in the room, so I asked, "Is Emma here?"

She did not answer. I assumed she had gone outdoors and joined the living children, or the ghost girl watched us from a corner and remained quiet.

The Basement

We clomped downstairs, and Erin led me to a door that was closed by the office. She entered the doorway and carried my ghost bag. I followed her down steps that were once used by the servants. At the bottom of the stairs there was a basement that also served as the winter kitchen when the Gilliams were alive. The summer kitchen was outside a few feet away, which would have been an inconvenience in the cold winter, but the winter kitchen would keep the upstairs warm.

Erin dropped the ghost bag on a table against the wall at the front of the house. I also put down the equipment I had.

Erin continued. "Over there is the kitchen, packed full of electronics, so people feel like they're being watched."

At that moment, we both heard something like a rock hit the floor between the ladder lying on its side by our feet and the wall.

Erin looked at me and whispered, "Was that you?"

My mouth went dry. "No."

We searched under the table and between the ladder and the wall, but we didn't find anything. Later, when I listened to the recording, I got an EVP right after our talking.

A couple of female voices blurted out, "That was us."

Erin told me she had to use one of the restrooms down in the basement, so I followed her. The restroom she stood in was much bigger than the other one in the hallway.

Facing me, she pointed at the wall to her left. "After a medium went to the restroom, she told me this wall made her feel uneasy. She had no reason for the feeling, except that it gave her an uncomfortable feeling."

The wall is between the restroom and the modern kitchen—had the electronics caused her discomfort or something else? Erin said the restroom used to be a storeroom. Who knew what had happened there as far back as when the slaves worked in this location.

I told her to stand in the restroom, so I could take a picture. Suddenly, a thin line of shadow crossed the small portion of wall between the restroom at my left and the entrance to the bigger one as I snapped the photograph. Just as quickly, it vanished. I tried to see if it had been me that made the shadow, duplicating what I'd just done, but no shadow reappeared. The toilet in the smaller restroom to my left began making flushing noises. After the shadow's appearance, neither toilet in either restroom had been used.

We did a short unsuccessful EVP session, then went to the ghost box.

I asked, "Who is here?"

A male voice replied: "Tom."

"Did I hear Tom?" No answer.

I asked, "Is Bishop here? He told me that he was a servant here."

Another male voice spoke: "Yep."

"Who else is here? Were you slaves of the Gilliams?"

A female voice: "Yes."

Erin indicated that the heat gun (a temperature sensor held like a gun and usually infrared) said it was growing colder in the area by my legs. My legs had been getting colder for the past couple of minutes.

"Are you making it colder?"

Some woman said: "No."

"Can you make it colder?"

A male voice answered: "Yes."

My feet and lower legs felt freezing, even though I wore pants, tennis shoes, and socks.

"What did you do here?" No answer.

"Did you cook?"

A woman said: "Yes."

A man said: "Served."

Then the box stopped scanning and reverted to a radio station. I shut it off and kept performing a straight EVP session. Erin said when she tested the heat gun twice by the wall at the back of the house and close to the modern kitchen, it went from 65° to 60°.

I tried a few more things. Finally, I said that if they wanted me to quit talking, to make a sound or push something. Later, I heard an EVP of a woman yelling: "Yes!"

We did one more thing. As mentioned earlier, when the investigators back in December were here, they played a game with dowsing rods and hidden objects in the basement. The spirits had to find the items by pointing with the rods. They got two out of five. Erin had hidden my ball that could light up in the left-hand side of the chest of drawers against the wall in the room. I proceeded to work with my dowsing rods. The rods in my hands stopped at the fireplace. Wrong. Erin asked them to try again. When I came to the chest, the rods moved and pointed at the chest of drawers. The ball was inside the drawer, so I took it out and packed it in my bag. I packed up the rest of the equipment, and we stomped back up the stairs to the first floor. I left Erin with another tour and went home.

Remember, the next time you take a walk or jog down to the dock behind this house after hours and glance back at the dining room windows on the first floor, you might see a woman in a blue gown standing there, staring at you. Please don't call the police on your cell phone. It's just one of Weston's ghosts keeping an eye on the house.

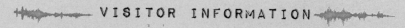

VISITOR INFORMATION

Weston Plantation
400 Weston Lane
Weston Lane and 21st Avenue
Hopewell VA 23860
804-458-4682

Monday to Saturday: 10 a.m. to 4:30 p.m.; Sunday: 1 p.m. to 4:30 p.m.

Tours: Adults $8.; Active Military $6.; Children under 12 free with adult; Groups of ten+ $6 per person

Appomattox Plantation House

I HAVE NEVER ADVOCATED WAR EXCEPT AS A MEANS OF PEACE.
—ULYSSES S. GRANT

Appomattox Plantation.

Is Appomattox Plantation house haunted, or not? Does the ghost of Ulysses S. Grant still wander around City Point, particularly near the cabin on the plantation land he used while there? And since it was used as a Civil War hospital, do any soldiers that died there still roam the area?

NOT TRUE!

One Civil War ghost story that is not true, but still told, concerned the house itself. Built in the late 1700s, the plantation house had expansions added later on by the Eppes family. It was abandoned by the Eppeses during the Civil War.

The legend tells of a nurse who hid a Union soldier in the wall of the basement when Confederate soldiers came to inspect the house. Unable to escape, he remained there even after the nurse had been taken away. Of course, he perished. It is said that he can be heard scratching at the walls to be let out. But the curator for the Petersburg National Battlefield never saw any proof for that story. He said that it sounded like something Edgar Allan Poe might have dreamed up.

Some History

Captain Francis Eppes acquired the land in 1635, by a land grant from Charles I. By the time his descendant, Dr. Richard Eppes (at the age of twenty) inherited the manor and the land in 1861, he'd received 2,200 acres and over a hundred slaves to tend to the place. He married a woman from Philadelphia, Pennsylvania, and they started a family.

Though he did not believe in succession, when Virginia seceded from the Union, he went ahead and joined the 3rd Virginia Cavalry when the War Between the States began. He left the army a year later, paying a replacement to fight for him in the war. He went to work as a civilian contract surgeon for the Confederate army in Petersburg. I learned that most planters were excluded from service and allowed to do this, as the Confederate government believed they needed to keep agricultural production going and to manage their slaves.

His family bolted when Union gunboats arrived in City Point in 1862, joining him in Petersburg. When the Siege of Petersburg began, Eppes slipped them out so they could go to his wife's family in Philadelphia. When Petersburg fell, he stayed behind to tend to the wounded as Robert E. Lee evacuated the Confederate forces from the city.

General Ulysses S. Grant took over the manor for his headquarters from June 15, 1864 until March 29, 1865. President Abraham Lincoln visited Grant there twice.

Dr. Eppes returned home in 1865. He scrounged up enough funds to buy back his plantation and his family returned home about 1866. The man lived out the rest of his days at the manor until his death in 1896.

A Visit

When I stopped at the plantation house to snap a picture of Grant's cabin, I did a short EVP and ghost box session. I waited until no one seemed to be around. On just the recording, I asked if Grant was still there, but no one answered me. When I asked if any of the Eppses still lingered, later at home as I listened, an EVP of a male voice said, "Me." When I used the ghost box and asked the same question, a male voice came across the scanning saying, "Grant." I'm not sure how Grant really sounded when he was alive or if this was someone else talking to point out that maybe because I was standing by Grant's cabin that Grant had been there at one time.

When I asked how they died, a young male voice said, "Pox."
I said, "So Grant is not lingering here, or is he?"

A voice replied, "Doesn't look like it." Bit of sarcasm there? I shut off the box, but not long after I did, I heard an EVP (when I listened later at home): "...... death." I wish I knew what the other two words were. But I heard "death" clear as day.

Come by and view the house and the outer buildings, plus the cabin Grant stayed in. Just don't be shocked if you run into one of the spirits of the Eppses family or even Grant himself. It's too nice a spot for even the dead not to appreciate.

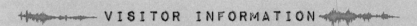 **VISITOR INFORMATION**

Appomattox Plantation House is located on the north side of VA Route 10, in Hopewell. Operated by the City Point Unit of the Petersburg National Battlefield, it is open daily for tours, 9 a.m. to 5 p.m., but is closed December 25 and Jan 1.

Ghosts of Evergreen Motel

```
LOST IN HIS OWN HORRIFIC CONTEMPLATIONS....
WHEN AT THE BED'S FOOT, CLOSE BESIDE THE POST,
HE VERILY BELIEVED HE SAW—A GHOST!
FROM EVERY PORE DISTILL'D A CLAMMY DEW,
QUAKED EVERY LIMBE—THE CANDLE, TOO...
THE ROOM WAS FILL'D WITH A SULPHUREOUS SMELL,
BUT WHERE THAT CAME FROM MASON COULD NOT TELL.
                          —THOMAS INGOLDSBY
```

On Mother's Day, Bill drove me to the Evergreen Motel in Hopewell. It is said that a ghost haunts one of the rooms of the motel or the building that stood there before the motel was opened.

In December 22, 1935, brake failure caused a Greyhound bus with fourteen people on board to crash on the drawbridge that was in place before the current concrete one, so drivers could cross from Chesterfield County into Hopewell. The bus plunged into thirty feet of icy water. There were no survivors. In fact, Charles Traina, who worked at Weston Plantation House, told me that when they brought up the bus, many of the bodies were frozen. It is said that one of the victim's spirit crawled up onto land and never left, remaining to haunt the hill after the motel had been built!

The legend states the bus accident happened on Christmas Eve in the 1930s. Afterwards, a newlywed couple appeared in an unconfirmed room on the first floor of the motel very close to the water. The couple, former guests at the hotel, appeared soaking wet. The problem with this story is that the bus was coming from Richmond, so how could they have been guests at the hotel? Had they driven down to Richmond just to catch the bus back to Hopewell? Not likely. Also, those who rent that particular motel room complain of one spirit, not two.

Another story is told about a visitor to the motel who was awakened by the feeling of a great weight upon his chest. He saw the figure above him and then it dissipated.

A Short Visit

While Bill waited inside the car, I grabbed my recorder, ghost box, and camera. After taking a few pictures, I began a session. I didn't get anything from the EVPs, except speedboats on the nearby river; however, the ghost box gave some results.

I asked, "Anybody here?"

Female voice: "Me."

"Did you die in the bus that went into the river? How many died?" Some words were obscured by a speedboat roaring by. "What year did the bus accident happen?"

A woman's voice answered: "1935."

"What is your name?"

A man's voice spoke up: "Luke." He went on to say his last name when I asked: "Ball."

The woman did not give her name. Who was this Luke then?

"Is there more than just one ghost here?"

Woman: "It's just me haunting."

Wow, that blew me away. Who was this female voice?

"What is the number of the room you haunt in the motel?"

The woman said either "nine" or "nineteen." I couldn't be sure.

I let the woman and the male know I was leaving them, and I thanked them for answering my questions. I put my stuff away and crawled into the passenger side of the Corolla. We drove away leaving the phantoms behind.

Next time you check into a room at the motel, don't be surprised if someone joins you in bed when you go to sleep. No one ever sleeps alone, not if the ghost can help it.

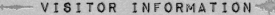

VISITOR INFORMATION

Riverside Suites (formerly Evergreen Motel)
711 West Randolph Road
Hopewell, VA 23860
804-458-8577

Did a Sea Serpent Once Swim the Appomattox River?

THEN THEY SAW ON THE WATER MANY A SNAKE-SHAPE,
STRONG SEA-SERPENTS EXPLORING THE MERE, AND WATER-
MONSTERS LYING ON THE SLOPES OF THE SHORE SUCH AS
THOSE THAT IN THE MORNING OFTEN ATTEND A PERILOUS
JOURNEY ON THE PATHS OF THE SEA, SERPENTS AND WILD
BEASTS.

—BEOWULF

When someone goes fishing, they expect to catch fish, maybe even a frog or two...but a sea serpent? That's what supposedly swam in the waters of the Appomattox River in Hopewell back in the 1980s.

Chessie was mostly seen in the Chesapeake Bay. For years, people reported sightings of a serpent-like creature. These reports were not unlike the legend of Nessie, the Loch Ness Monster. She even made the news in the late 1960s.

Witnesses say the creature seen in Hopewell could have been twenty-five to forty feet in length, dark, with no limbs, fins, or distinguishable details on its oval head. It was no more than a foot across in width.

It appeared when Chessie decided to leave the bay and swim upriver to Hopewell. A woman caught sight of the creature after she had gone to dinner with her husband at the Harbor Light Restaurant. She noticed something strange with a long, undulating body that swam closer and closer. It matched descriptions of the beast seen in the Chesapeake Bay.

A manatee has been seen in the Appomattox River not too long ago. Could this be what was mistaken for a sea serpent in the 1980s? Sharks have also been seen swimming in the nearby James River, and someone told me he'd found shark's teeth in the sand by the Appomattox as a kid. What else could swim from the sea to Hopewell?

Since the 1980s, the creature has not been seen in the river or on the Chesapeake Bay.

But the next time you go boating on the river or plan to go fishing, take care. Chessie might still be living beneath the water.

ENON, ETTRICK-MATOAC AND CHESTER

FOR WHO CAN WONDER THAT MAN SHOULD FEEL A VAGUE
BELIEF IN TALES OF DISEMBODIED SPIRITS WANDERING
THROUGH THOSE PLACES WHICH THEY ONCE DEARLY
AFFECTED. WHEN HE HIMSELF, SCARCELY LESS SEPARATED
FROM HIS OLD WORLD THAN THEY, IS FOR EVER LINGERING
UPON PAST EMOTIONS AND BYGONE TIMES, AND HOVERING,
THE GHOST OF HIS FORMER SELF, ABOUT THE PLACES
AND PEOPLE THAT WARMED HIS HEART OF OLD?

—CHARLES DICKENS

Being part of Chesterfield County, and close to Petersburg, Hopewell, and Colonial Heights, I decided to add some haunted spots in Enon, Ettrick-Matoaca, and Chester. Situated between the James and Appomattox Rivers, this area is rich in history and outdoor experiences.

Enon uses alligators as mascots for their schools and volunteer fire department. There are no real alligators stalking the area—not even a legend about them. But Enon *is* a very swampy area.

Scottish merchant Neil Buchanan founded Ettrick in 1765. It became home to the Ettrick Manufacturing Company and operated along the Appomattox River. The mill produced flour, cottonseed oil, cotton, silk, and corn. Between 1830 and 1840, Ettrick's economic prosperity gave rise to its first urban residential settlement. These areas are now known as Main, Light, Pannil, Totty, Court, and Jackson Streets. The village of Ettrick had approximately 830 residents by 1859.

In neighboring Matoaca, the construction of a textile mill in 1836 spawned a settlement of approximately 500 people. The Matoaca Manufacturing Company operated grist mills and manufactured paper and cotton.

Today, Ettrick has Virginia State University, and the Ettrick-Matoaca Historical Society holds their annual Celtic Festival in April. It has its own library branch of Chesterfield County and the Ettrick-Matoaca Volunteer Rescue Squad.

The "downtown" part of Chester was a stop on the Richmond and Petersburg Railroad. The Chester Station was the scene of a battle during the American Civil War. Today, Chester has a village green where many shops, the Chester branch of the Chesterfield County Library, and restaurants are situated. During spring to fall, a farmer's market is held on Saturdays along with Chester Fest and other events. Chester is served by the local newspaper *The Village News*. The area was damaged by Hurricane Isabel in 2003.

But do these areas of Chesterfield County have spirits? Keep reading to discover for yourself.

Screamersville

ONE THING I HATE IS PEOPLE SCREAMING AT ME.

—MARIO LEMIEUX

Here is an interesting story that Charles Traina at Weston told me concerning Enon. There is a section of State Road that is called Screamersville. Some of the people buried in the area are freed slaves from the post-Civil War era who had settled in the town. At its peak in the 1940s, the isolated village was home to about eighty residents along State Avenue. The community began to disappear when Interstate 295 cut through in the 1980s. Many of the aging residents were dying, and younger ones moved away. A part of Screamersville is now Rivermont Station, an upscale apartment complex, and Rivermont Landing townhouses and condominiums.

One story behind the area's name comes from the freed slaves, who were poor and lived hard lives. They learned how to party and make the best of their circumstances—a lot of screaming and revelry being a result. Another theory for the name involves the lack of modern conveniences, like telephones, so people hollered from porch to porch to communicate with each other. Now the area is populated by modern houses and condos, but there are a few graveyards that reveal another possible theory: the dead are screaming from their graves.

Still another tale told is that the slaves were beaten by their overseers; however, if freed slaves lived in this area, how could this be? One last theory that suggests the village may have gotten its name from the Union hospital, at the nearby Point of Rocks, where, during the Civil War, soldiers' limbs were amputated without anesthetic.

Whatever the reason behind the name—ghostly or realistic—the next time you drive through this part of Enon and hear screaming, ignore it. It's just past residents still communicating the only way they know how.

VISITOR INFORMATION

Screamersville, Virginia, has a Facebook page:
www.facebook.com/pages/Screamersville-
Virginia/109154239108661?fref=ts.

There are many town and areas in the United States with odd or scary names. To find others, check here:
www.thejetpacker.com/66-towns-and-cities-with-scary-names.

Supernatural Tales of Ettrick-Matoaca

NATURE IS A HAUNTED HOUSE—BUT ART IS A HOUSE THAT
TRIES TO BE HAUNTED.

—EMILY DICKINSON

A Ghostly Experience

One legend tells of a woman who used to have paranormal experiences as a child, but hadn't had them for years. All that changed when she moved into a house in Matoaca.

First, she breathed in a strong odor of bacon cooking when no one was cooking. It made her nauseous. The next day, she got up at four in the morning and padded over to her dresser when she heard a child speaking very loud and clear right behind her! At first, she thought it was one of her own kids, but then she remembered they'd gone with their friends to Virginia Beach the day before. She was alone in the house at the time.

Haunted School

Strange things occurred at the former Matoaca High School. Cold chills would be felt, lights would turn on and off, doors would shake and bang, and other noises would be heard. The story goes that when the building was a high school, a girl who attended there was involved in one of the school's plays. On the night of a performance, stage lights fell on her and she died. The auditorium was then haunted by her spirit.

No activity has been reported since the building was converted into a middle school.

Dellwood Plantation

Dellwood Plantation is a bed and breakfast in Ettrick-Matoaca along Woodpecker Road.

The building's history begins with John Winston Jones. He graduated from the Law School of The College of William and Mary in 1813. After a few years of practicing law, he became the prosecuting attorney for the Fifth Judicial Circuit Court in Chesterfield County in 1818. He was a member of the State Constitutional Convention in 1829 and 1830 and did a stint as Speaker of the

House of Representatives from 1843–1845, and was a member of the Virginia House of Delegates in 1846.

John W. Jones owned Dellwood and Woodson Plantations in Chesterfield County and Clifton Hill, known today as Fort Clifton. He married Harriet Boisseau and they raised three children at Dellwood: Mary Winston, James Boisseau, and Alexander. John passed away in 1848 and was interred at the cemetery on Dellwood Plantation. His wife inherited the plantation and, in turn, their son, James B.

Following in his father's footsteps, James attended and graduated from The College of William and Mary Law School. He married Anne Crawley on October 13, 1842, at Dellwood Plantation. Dellwood remained in his possession during the Civil War. Together with Major Augustus Drewry of Drewry's Bluff, Jones financed the heavy artillery for the Battle at Drewry's Bluff fought on May 15, 1862. This battle saved Richmond by fending off Union vessels. During the War Between the States, Dellwood Plantation was open to sick and injured soldiers (both Union and Confederate).

It has been said that someone staying there awoke in the night to a voice coming from someplace in their room...but no one was there.

Paranormal Chester

GOD! WHOSE HAND WAS I HOLDING?

—SHIRLEY JACKSON

Lonely Ghost: Civil War Soldier

This ghost story, set in the Chester area, was given to me by Charles Traina of Weston Plantation House. He had been told about the ghost by someone from a utility business on Jefferson Davis Highway in Chester. It involves a Civil War soldier who had been shot and then rested against a large tree—maybe as the last thing he would do. He propped his rifle against the tree and expired.

Years later, he has been seen by many people, particularly the owners of an old house built on the land. By use of a metal detector, his rifle was found still propped against the tree about ten years ago. It had been covered by overgrown grass and weeds. The bones of the soldier have never been found, though (at least not that Traina knew).

Does the soldier still haunt the spot, or is he finally at rest? Good question.

Ghost Lady in the Mirror

Tamara Evans grew up in a Chester home. In this home, something paranormal happened to her now-adult son Brandon, when he was a young boy. He had been taking a bath and soaping up his hair into spikes when the bathroom mirror fogged up. When the glass cleared, the boy looked up at an old lady in a floral-patterned dress staring back at him. This scared him, and he bolted from the bathroom and down the stairs to find his mother to describe the lady to her. She recognized her aunt from her own childhood. When she had been just ten years old in 1956, her Aunt Pokey had died in the basement. Though she'd never appeared to Tamara or anyone else, she decided to show herself to young Brandon. To this day, Brandon never talks about it to anyone.

Swift Creek Mill Theatre

WITH THEATRE, YOU HAVE TO BE READY FOR ANYTHING.
—WILLEM DEFOE

Swift Creek Mill Theatre.

Theatres for years have stories of hauntings about them. Whether due to actors or crew dying or the history of the land the building is set on, theatres can offer more than a night of a play and sometimes dinner. It can offer patrons the dead!

Located at 17401 Jefferson Davis Highway with a Colonial Heights address and yet connected to neighboring Chesterfield County, too, the Swift Creek Mill Theatre offers people great plays and even dinner beforehand, if one so desires.

The playhouse in the beginning was a gristmill. Gristmills grind grain into flour. Henry Randolph I built it adjacent to his plantation in 1663. Besides being operated as a plantation mill, it also acted as a merchant mill and remained Randolph's Mill until 1804. That was when William Rowlett bought it and changed the name to Rowlett's Mill. He operated it until 1852. Then the Swift Creek Mill Manufacturing Company bought the property and restructured it.

What people see when they come to the theatre that dates back to historic times is the brick portion of the building, windows, and its doors. The stone ground floor as well as the limestone basement can be dated back to the original building.

Then the War Between the States happened. The mill became the center of a battle on May 10, 1864. Union troops tried to cross Swift Creek to disrupt the Confederate lines. They repelled the Rebels back across the creek and burned railroad ties to ruin the rails. The Confederate troops pushed the Union back across the next day and repaired the lines.

The war ended and the mill became Schmidt's Distillery to be used as a gristmill and a distillery for corn whiskey until 1872. Several owners later, Amanda Percival bought it and operated it until 1959.

It was in 1965 that three families bought the property so they could bring a live professional theatre to the area. They kept the place as it was, but transformed the mill into a dinner theatre. The playhouse is still there after forty-nine years.

Like many other theatres, there are tales of it being haunted. One story found in some old records at Chesterfield County Courthouse tells of a man who hung himself from the rafters when it was just a mill. It is said he still roams the building. Another makes claim of a young female child apparition seen in various parts of the place. Others reveal shadowy figures as well as voices heard—especially in the basement. At one point, a paranormal team was brought in and got EVPs.

Next time you attend a play at Swift Creek Mill Theatre and stop to comb your hair in the restroom, don't be frightened if you see someone enter and then walk through a wall. What good theatre doesn't have real spirit...I mean the haunting kind.

VISITOR INFORMATION

Swift Creek Mill Theatre
17401 Jefferson Davis Highway
South Chesterfield, VA 23834
804-748-5203 for tickets
www.swiftcreekmill.com

From Interstate 95, take Exit 58B onto Woods Edge Road. Travel 0.7 mile to US Route 1. Travel south on US Route 1 (Jefferson Davis Highway) 1.5 miles to Swift Creek Mill Theatre on the left. The entrance is just before the bridge crossing Swift Creek.

Falling Creek Ironworks Park

BEFORE THE END OF TWO MOONES THERE SHOULD NOT BE
AN ENGLISHMAN IN ALL THEIR COUNTRIES.

—OPECHANCANOUGH

Entrance into the park.

Located at 6407 Jefferson Davis Highway, there is the site of the first ironworks in English North America: Falling Creek Ironworks Park, a part of Chesterfield County. It may also be haunted, thanks to the 1622 Indian Massacre, along with modern-day murders. Jefferson Davis is considered to be an unsafe area at this time.

Captain Bluett selected the site for iron production in 1619. But two years later, a second expedition, led by John Berkley, his son Maurice, and twenty ironworkers arrived at Falling Creek. Berkley had written to the Virginia Company that he would produce iron for them by spring of the following year. Sadly, the death of Powhatan and the ascension of Opechancanough as paramount chief brought about terrible things that stopped this from ever happening. Falling Creek Ironworks was one of the stops that the Powhatan Indians included in their colony-wide attack and

Timber in the creek that a storm brought up and experts believe is part of the ironworks.

massacre on March 22, 1622. There are two stories of survivors of the massacre: one says that only two children lived; the other states that everyone was killed. Several attempts to restore the ironworks occurred, but with no success.

The park has a list of those who died, and I will post it in this book. Reading this list after I returned home, I had a surprise. I had done a ghost box session after the tour, and the name I was given, after asking for a name of anyone who died during the massacre, was the first and last name of the gentleman at the top of the list! (I will talk more about these recordings later in this chapter.)

A list of those who died, including the spirit who gave me his first and last name, is on this sign.

Archibald Cary built a forge on the north side of Falling Creek in 1760. The forge proved to be unprofitable, so he turned his attention to a grist mill that had been destroyed during the American Revolution. This finery forge operation had a varied history. The land returned to grist milling. There are referenced sources that lay claim to continuous operations through to 1781 when Benedict Arnold had it burned to the ground. Rebuilt in the 1850s by John Watkins, it was active until about 1906.

Roger Bensley developed Bensley Village in the 1930s. He acquired Falling Creek as part of his holdings for the first Bon Air type of planned community south of the James. He asserted that he found several structures when bulldozing that might be the ironworks, but never produced a map to show where they were located.

A Visit

I parked by the field where Native Indians reenacted dances in their ceremonial finery; people were dressed in costumes of the 1600s and 1700s, and people in modern clothing behind tables explained about organizations or the history of the area. I took a few photos and wandered around until the first tour of the Falling Creek Ironworks Park began. Archeologist Lyle Brown spoke to us about what happened on the land 394 years ago until today. Mr. Brown works for the Falling Creek Ironworks Foundation.

After I took the tour, I wandered down the trail hoping to find a good spot to do both an EVP and a ghost box session. I let others from the tour pass me as I stopped by some trees and bushes on the trail. I started the EVP session first. I didn't get anything. No voices or sounds other than normal voices of the living and sounds from the birds, creek, and vehicles on the nearby Jefferson Davis Highway. I decided to try the ghost box.

"Are any spirits here?"

"Yes." It was a man's voice with an accent. It wasn't modern American or someone who didn't speak English as we speak it today.

"Were you killed during the Indian massacre in 1622?"

"Yes."

Another man with a Hispanic accent said: "No."

"How many perished?"

"Twenty-one." Later, after everything was written down for this chapter, I checked the photo I took of the sign in the park with the names of who had died and how many. Twenty-one was correct!

"Can you give me your name?"

"Philip."

"A last name I can verify, please?"

"Barnes." As I read what I wrote from hearing on the recording, I checked the photo again with the names and found a Philip Barnes at the top of the list!

I asked if there were any modern spirits connected to the Falling Creek Apartments next door—this because there are many gang- and drug-related crimes there, and I wondered if any deaths occurred at the apartments or in the locked park after dark.

I said, "Espanola?" Suddenly a spattering of Spanish could be heard from the box. It sounded like it came from a Spanish radio station—or maybe from those who had lived next door at Falling Creek Apartments and died there. It stopped as suddenly as it had begun.

I walked out of the park, stopped at the highway, and ran across Jefferson Davis Highway to get to the park with the crumbling remains of the bridge. I did an EVP session and snapped a few pictures. Later, when listening to the EVP session, I found nothing on the recording. Nothing was in any of the photos, either.

It is said that terrible tragedies cause hauntings, such as plane crashes, where wars happen, etc. So, it would be assumed that a massacre would leave something connected to the land—even 394 years later. It seems that those who came to the New World to produce iron, only to perish horribly, still wait to tell their story. Maybe telling me their tale has helped them to move on. Then again, maybe not.

Someone at Chesterfield County's Parks and Recreation main office told me when she was a child and lived around Jefferson Davis Highway, they used to tease other kids about the haunted house that occupied the land where the Falling Creek Apartments now sit. This made me wonder if the place had been haunted because of the past residents of the house, or due to the 1622 Massacre.

For a great tour of the Falling Creek Iron Works, check it out during the event held there in March. Just don't be surprised as you walk along the trail alongside the creek and see a gentleman dressed in clothing from the 1600s. He's not a reenactor—not when he dissipates before your eyes!

VISITOR INFORMATION

Falling Creek Iron Works
6407 Jefferson Davis Highway
North Chesterfield, VA 23234
www.fallingcreekironworks.org

The site is open for tours by reservation only. Find out how to make a reservation or the date for annual Falling Creek Ironworks tour (held in March usually) at www.fallingcreekironworks.org. Also, call for park information: 804-748-1623 and tour information: 804-751-4946.

Battery Dantzler Park

IN A BATTLE ALL YOU NEED TO MAKE YOU FIGHT IS A
LITTLE HOT BLOOD AND THE KNOWLEDGE THAT IT'S MORE
DANGEROUS TO LOSE THAN TO WIN.
— GEORGE BERNARD SHAW

Battery Dantzler.

My friend Ann Eacho-Krampf and I visited Battery Dantzler on Sunday, June 16, 2013. We were waiting for a couple of other paranormal investigators (Leonard Price and Julia Ogle) to join us, but we decided to walk into the park and check it out prior to their arrival.

Battery Dantzler is an official park of Chesterfield County established just in time for the 150th anniversary of the Civil War.

Confederate authorities considered locating the main defensive James River battery to block the Union navy's approach to Richmond in 1862. They chose Drewry's Bluff instead, because they feared Union forces would bypass this position by cutting a canal through the river bend at Dutch Gap. The landing of Union Major General Benjamin F. Butler's army on the James River at Bermuda Hundred in May 1864 prompted the construction of this fortification. It was named Battery Dantzler in honor of Colonel Olin Miller Dantzler, 22nd South Carolina Infantry, who was killed trying to take Fort Dutton on June 2, 1864. Battery Dantzler anchored the northern end of the Howlett Line of earthworks across the Bermuda Hundred peninsula from the James River south to the Appomattox River.

It played a major role in keeping the Union navy from reaching Richmond. In January 1865, armed with two ten-inch columbiads, a seven-inch Brooke rifle, and one ten-inch mortar, the Johnston Artillery under Captain B.J. Eppes manned the site. By April 2, 1865, the battery was abandoned.

The fort was briefly occupied by Union infantry on June 16, 1864, when Confederate General P.G.T. Beauregard pulled his men out of Bermuda Hundred to defend against Grant's first threats at Petersburg. The guns at Dantzler were dismounted and buried where they remained hidden until the Confederates retook the position the following day. They quickly remounted the guns just in time when, on June 21, the fort exchanged fire with Union vessels in the James River.

Still waiting on the other investigators (and in 90° heat!), we took pictures and did an EVP session as we walked along the path. We also walked over a wooden bridge and looked in the wooded area.

We finally saw Leonard and Julia as they pulled into the parking spot next to our two vehicles and got out. They gathered what equipment they planned to use, and then, we all went to the viewing platform to investigate.

Ann turned on video and I had my EMF meter on. We began an EVP session.

"Any spirit involved with the Civil War with us?" No answer.

"What year did you die?" Still nothing.

"What's your name?" Not a word. I did not know I hadn't gotten any replies at the time—not until I listened later at home. At this point, either no spirit stayed in the battery or they remained quiet.

Then, as I listened to the recording, I heard this weird noise I could not figure out. It didn't come from sounds of vehicles on the roads nearby, trains, or anything else I would recognize. I heard myself ask a few more questions, then another sound, like a wind blowing and leaves scattering. There was no wind or breeze that day, which would have been really nice with the heat. Everything was still. The only leaves would be kicked by *our* feet, but none of us moved. So I wondered what was this? Seconds later, it was gone.

I decided to use my dowsing rods to see what we might get. Maybe being from the Civil War, they might be more comfortable using them over speaking into the recorders. I still left my recorder on, though.

"Have you fought in the War Between the States? Cross the rods if you did. Don't cross if you did not."

As the rods crossed, my recorder picked up a loud ping that I swore I did not hear live back then.

"Uncross the rods, please." The rods swung open.

"Are both Northern and Southern troops here with us? Cross the rods if so." The rods made an x.

"Uncross the rods." They parted.

"Thank you. Are you still fighting the war? Cross the rods if you are, or don't cross them if you are not." They crossed.

"Thank you."

Ann spoke up. "You know, you don't have to stay here."

At this point, I got an EVP of a male voice. "Yes."

Yes, he had to stay? Or yes, he knew he could go if he wanted to?

Ann continued, "Cross if you want to go to the other side."

The rods stayed stationary.

She persisted, "So you don't want to go?"

The rods did not move.

She said, "Well, I can understand you wanting to stay here. It is pretty."

I put away the rods and brought out the ghost box. I turned it on, set it to AM, and scanned as I explained they could use the scanning radio waves to speak to us live.

I asked, "How many spirits are with us?"

I got a male voice that sounded like "seven."

"Can I get a name?"

A male voice answered: "Harrick." (I am not sure of the spelling, so hopefully this is right!)

"Do you want to talk to us?"

Same male voice again. "No."

There was nothing more, except the whistle of a train that I'd heard live in the distance. The soldiers never said anything after that.

Want to find a nice spot to check out Civil War history and relax? Chesterfield County has a new park you might like. The river is not far away, and it is a pretty spot. Don't be surprised at dusk as you make your way out to your vehicle if you see a figure in a Civil War uniform. You're not the only one enjoying the park.

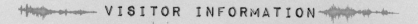

VISITOR INFORMATION

Battery Dantzler Park
1820 Battery Dantzler Road
Chester, VA 23836
Park Information, 804-748-1623 Tour Information, 804-751-4946

The park is open sunrise to sunset daily and is free to the public. There is a reconstructed viewing platform that is handicapped accessible. There is a historical marker at the park as well as a Virginia Civil War Trails interpretive sign.

Visit www.chesterfieldhistory.com/CivilWar/BatteryDantzler.html for more information.

Parker's Battery

WAR IS CRUELTY. THERE IS NO USE TRYING TO REFORM
IT. THE CRUELER IT IS, THE SOONER IT WILL BE OVER.
—WILLIAM TECUMSEH SHERMAN

Parker's Battery, at 1801 Ware Bottom Spring Road in Chester, is a well-preserved example of the Confederate defenses known as the Howlett Line. The prominent battery went by "The Boy Company," and was comprised of men from the city of Richmond led by Captain William Parker. Under his leadership, this battery forged a strong record on many of the Civil War battlefields. Before here, many fought Second Manassas (Bull Run), Sharpsburg (Antietam), and Gettysburg. Though most were at least twenty-five years old, some lads between the ages fourteen and nineteen also joined. Infantry trenches ran from south of the James River to the Appomattox River, and they supported artillery positions along the line. From mid-June 1864 forward, Parker's Battery artillerymen were involved in frequent duels with Federal positions less than one mile east. Confederate forces occupied this site until the fall of Petersburg in April 2, 1865. They retreated and followed Lee to Appomattox.

Members of the company purchased this property after the war and held reunions. When the last members of the company died, the land was donated to the National Park Service, in the 1930s. The site features a walking trail with several interpretive signs and is open from dawn until dusk.

Ghostly legends tell of voices coming from the earthworks when there is no one around. Sometimes, if a figure is seen, it quickly disappears.

The Investigation:
JUNE 16, 2013

On Sunday, June 16, 2013, after investigating Drewry's Bluff and Battery Dantzler, my friends and fellow investigators Ann Eacho-Krampf, Leonard Price, Julia Ogle, and I visited Parker's Battery. We stopped by the sign out front, and I noticed this was an anniversary date for the battle. I remembered how people said more supernatural occurrences happened on the anniversary date of a haunted spot, so I hoped this would be true today.

We stopped near the end of the wooden bridge that led into the park to do an EVP session, and I used my ghost box for some part of that. Later, after I got home and listened, I found the recordings from Drewry's Bluff and Battery Dantzler still intact, but nothing of Parker's Battery. It was like paranormal forces had struck that part from my recorder. I emailed the others, and they had gotten some recordings, but I didn't. The photographs developed okay. Why not the EVPs and ghost box session? It was all very bizarre to say the least.

The Investigation:
JUNE 16, 2014

I returned a year later. After Bill parked our car in the small parking lot of Parker's Battery, I grabbed my EMF meter, recorder, camera, ghost box, and stepped out. He remained in the vehicle, but I proceeded to the wooden bridge that would take me into the park.

My EMF meter had four lights showing when I was outside the park; but, like the last time I'd been there, I assumed that might have been due to the electrical wiring above and the nearby warehouses. It dropped down to three lights once I stopped at the part of the bridge closest to the path. I switched on my recorder and did an EVP session first. I heard nothing when I listened at home.

I turned to the ghost box next. I hoped I would get something, as this was the second day of the anniversary of the battle.

"Is there anybody here with me?"

A young male voice channeled through the box: "Me!"

"Are you with the Boy Company? Can you say y—"

The scanning shut off.

I set it to scan again. "I was just trying to be sure you're with the Boy Company. You're not?"

"Boy Company." Got an answer there.

"Is Captain William Parker here? Also, I heard you had boys as young as fourteen in the company. Any young men here? Give me some names."

I heard: "Seay."

I spoke again, "Anybody else? I am Pamela. What is your name?"

"Seay." (When I was home, after listening, I found a site with all the names shown on the sign at the end of the park and printed them to double-check. I found what sounded like "Say" to me at the time I heard it, but it was spelled "Seay" on the sign.

"Did I hear Seay?"

"Yes."

I asked the spirits how near they were.

One said: "Here."

I said, "You can keep talking to me, but I am turning off my ghost box and will just use my recorder. Is that all right?

A boyish voice said: "Yes, please," before I shut off the ghost box.

I wandered up the path to the first earthworks in another part of the park, taking pictures along the way with my camera. I thought I heard footsteps behind me for a second. Had I? (Later, as I listened to the recording, I did hear the footsteps.)

I came upon the first earthworks. I had seen them covered in leaves in the winter, but today grass and plants costumed them. I snapped a few pictures of them and the woods on each side. My EMF meter had lowered to two lights, but now had three. I switched on the ghost box.

I began by telling the spirits not to follow me home, but to remain here when I was ready to go. Then I asked, "Is Captain William Parker here?"

A deep male voice came over my box. "Captain."

Was it Parker? Even though he hadn't died in battle here, maybe he'd returned here after his death.

"Did Captain Parker ever come back here?"

"No."

This might not be him then. I asked, "What is your name, sir?"

I thought I heard Miller. (Later, looking at the list of who had fought here, I found two last names of Miller listed.)

I spoke again. "Anyone here leave a girlfriend or wife behind?"

"Yes."

"Anyone leave their parents behind when they went to war?"

Several young-sounding male voices answered: "Yes!"

I said, "Thank you for your answers. It is hard leaving loved ones behind."

A man said: "Yes, Ma'am."

"Is this the Boy Company?"

Same voice answered. "Yes."

"Can some of the boys speak? What were your ages?"

I think I got two ages from two different voices. "Thirty." The other said, "Sixteen."

Union troops had fought at nearby Ware Church Battlefield, too, and died there, so I decided to ask to see if only Confederates were here with me. "Confederate?"

A young man said: "Confederate."

"Thank you very much for your replies, I am going to leave you now. Goodbye."

The ghost box scanning shut off. I guess that was their goodbye to me. I headed back up the path.

As I got halfway back, I swore I heard more footsteps behind me on the path and alongside me. I thought I heard whispering to the right of me as well. Animals? I felt like I was being watched. I halted, turned around, and snapped a couple of pictures that whitened, unlike others I took earlier and after. It felt like a crowd stood up along the path staring at me, with more from both sides of the woods. I started to grow more uncomfortable than I already felt. I walked faster. Before I left, I shot a few more pictures. Later at home, I was suspicious of the blue outside the trees in the park, even though Bill said it was the sky. The unearthly blue was not where the sky would be in a photo, being too close to the ground. I enlarged the picture to draw closer, until I saw the top part of a figure wearing a uniform and with a cap upon its head.

Boys as young as fourteen went to war and, at Parker's Battery, some of their spirits still hang around. It is heartbreaking that they may not have made it home to their families. So don't be surprised when you visit the park, if you hear boyish laughter—it's just the boys of The Boy Company.

See the figure in the blue light in this close up? He is next to the thin trunk of a tree. The figure had to be in the field outside of the park. Does that mean the rest of the blue light is also the dead soldiers of the Boy Company?

VISITOR INFORMATION

Parker's Battery
1801 Ware Bottom Spring Road
Chester, VA 23831
804-226-1981
www.chesterfieldhistory.com/CivilWar/ParkersBattery.html

Parker's Battery is a United States government owned park and features a walking trail with several interpretive signs. The park closes at sunset.

Ware Bottom Church Battlefield Park

WE TALKED THE MATTER OVER AND COULD HAVE SETTLED
THE WAR IN THIRTY MINUTES HAD IT BEEN LEFT TO US.
—UNKNOWN CONFEDERATE SOLDIER
REFERENCING A MEETING HE HAD WITH A UNION
SOLDIER BETWEEN THE LINES

It was on May 20, 1864, that 10,000 Confederate troops under General P.G.T. Beauregard attacked Butler's Bermuda Hundred line near Ware Bottom Church. As they drove Butler's advanced pickets back, the Confederates constructed the Howlett Line bottling up the Federals at Bermuda Hundred. This became known as "the cork in the bottle." Thanks to the Confederate victories at Proctor's Creek and Ware Bottom Church, Beauregard was able to send strong reinforcements for Lee's army in time for the fighting at Cold Harbor.

I set my GPS with the address on Old Hundred Road, and the voice led me to turn left off Jefferson Davis Highway (I was coming from Colonial Heights). I drove until the voice announced I had reached the address. One side has businesses with several addresses; however, none of them were 1700 Old Bermuda Hundred Road. Across the road from the buildings was tree-covered land. Had this spot of land been the battlefield? I left the area and drove to Parker's Battery.

Looking up the battlefield again, I found I had the wrong address and, on Mother's Day, Bill placed the right one in his smart phone's GPS and drove to the park. The park was not open and no one was around, so I got out of the car, bringing my digital recorder, ghost box, and my camera. I took a few pictures, and then began the session. Nothing on the EVP one; however, I did get a couple of direct answers from a male voice though the ghost box.

I asked, "Any Civil War soldiers here?"

"Yes."

"South or North?"

Male voice: "North."

"I am going to leave now, so thank you for talking to me."

Male: "Bye."

"Oh. Good-bye."

At that moment, it felt as if someone stood behind me, then went up and over me into the woods. My hair stood on end, and a chill ran through me. I backed away and returned to the car.

Bill asked me what was next, and we drove off. I didn't look back. If I had, would I have seen something standing at the beginning of the path, watching us?

When the park opens, go there, walk the path, and get to know its history. But be forewarned, the history is still there.

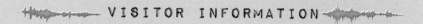

VISITOR INFORMATION

Ware Bottom Church
1600 Old Bermuda Hundred Road
Chester, VA 23831
804-751-4946
www.chesterfieldhistory.com/CivilWar/WareBottom.html

The park is owned by Chesterfield County Parks and Recreation and closes at sunset.

Conclusion

Thus ends this book. Petersburg has so much history behind it that it cannot fail to prove it is one of the Commonwealth's most prominently paranormal active areas—except for my chapter that proves not all old buildings are haunted, even if historical. But even with that, there are many more apparitions of all types that make the Tri-Cities area a very spooky place to live and visit.

Take time to drop in on the restaurants, museums, cemeteries, attractions, and parks that add to the many layers of Petersburg, Colonial Heights, Hopewell, and the nearby counties. Eat the food, check out the history, and come play in the parks...but be forewarned. Not just the living exists there. These are also the stomping grounds for the unseen, and they can't wait to haunt you.

Be prepared to be scared!

Bibliography

Abugel, Jeffrey. *Edgar Allan Poe's Petersburg: The Untold Story of the Raven in the Cockade City.* Charleston, SC: The History Press, 2013.

Barrow, Charles Kelly, J. H. Segar, and R. B. Rosenburg. *Black Confederates.* Gretna, Louisiana: Pelican Publishing Company, 2011.

Hauck, Dennis William. *Haunted Places, The National Directory.* New York, New York: Penguin Books, 2002.

Kinney, Pamela K. *Haunted Richmond, Virginia.* Atglen, Pennsylvania: Schiffer Publishing, Ltd., 2007.

Kinney, Pamela K. *Haunted Richmond II.* Atglen, Pennsylvania: Schiffer Publishing, Ltd., 2012.

Kinney, Pamela K. *Haunted Virginia: Legends, Myths and True Tales.* Atglen, Pennsylvania: Schiffer Publishing, Ltd., 2009

Lee, Marguerite DuPont. *Virginia Ghosts.* Berryville, Virginia: Virginia Book Company, 1966.

Nesbitt, Mark. *Civil War Ghost Trails.* Stackpole Books: Mechanicsburg, Pennsylvania, 2012.

Nichols, Janet Bernard. *Sketch of Old Blandford Church.* Petersburg, Virginia: The Ladies Memorial Association, 2007.

Taylor, L. B. *Civil War Ghosts of Virginia.* Williamsburg, Virginia: self published 1996.

Taylor, L. B. *The Ghosts of Richmond.* Williamsburg, Virginia: self published 1985.

Taylor, L. B. *The Ghosts of Virginia Volume II.* Williamsburg, Virginia: self published 1996.

Taylor, L. B. *The Ghosts of Virginia Volume XII.* Williamsburg, Virginia: self published 1996.

Taylor, L. B. *Monsters of Virginia: Mysterious Creatures in the Old Dominion.* Mechanicsburg, Pennsylvania: Stackpole Books, 2012.

Acknowledgments

I'd like to acknowledge those who helped me in learning about the history and ghostly lore of Petersburg, Dinwiddie, Prince George, the city of Hopewell, the city of Colonial Heights, and even nearby Chester and Ettrick-Matoaca in Chesterfield County.

I would like to thank Susan Schwartz for her invaluable assistance in being my beta reader for this book.

Thank you also goes to my son, Christopher Truesdale, for any invaluable insights on any of the photos and video I prepared for the book.

I am adding a special thank you to all who donated to my cat Shade's medical bill when I set up a Crowdfunding page or shared it on your walls when you couldn't afford to. Without all your support during that difficult time, I wouldn't have been able to work on my manuscript. Thanks go to Terri Pray and Final Sword Productions, Sandra Hughes, Jan Kozlowski, Becky Brunton, Suanne Brady, Brandon Blackmoor, Glenn Gibson, Jamie Hanrahan, Karen Snaultbelt, Faye Newsham, Liz Albitz, Michael Vann, Rene Enders, Tracy Delisle, Linda Sullivan, Steven Stockbarger, Julie Scharff, Lisa Harrigan, Les Wheatley, Gloria Kleckner, Wendy Norman, Elizabeth Garner, Denice Girardeau, Mary Ussery-White, Susan Wickham, Teresa Labbee, Cynthya Petzen, Judy Chirila, Jesse Braxton, Genie Hillen, Giselle Marks, Gina Farago, Donna Dube, Gia Eirich, Susan Schwartz, Kathryn Elms, Nora Mai, Vivian Perry, Chris Impink, Kellie Hamilton, Jeanine Elizalde, and Stepahanie St. Clair.

Thanks to Carol Smith, Julia Ogle, and Leonard Price for joining me at The Bistro at Market and Grove and even Peter Jones Trading Post beforehand, and helping me investigate. Thank you also to DJ Payne of Wabi Sabi, Sid Scott of Blue Willow Tea Room, Russ Johnson, Jeff Abugel of Hiram Haines Coffee and Ale House, Violet Bank Museum, and Weston Plantation House, who let me conduct an investigation in addition to the interviews at their various places. Thank you to Weston Plantation House's tour guide, Erin Winn, who led me through the house that Sunday afternoon and braved the spirits with me. I'd like to thank the United States government for preserving the battlefields I investigated for this book—it's not just the ghosts, but the history they have saved for generations to come. Thank you to Chesterfield County for saving the history and creating the Civil War parks and Falling Creek Ironworks Park. Thank you to those who gave me stories—those that happened to you, or that you'd heard of.

And thank you to my readers. You are all ghost hunters in my eyes.

Index

Other Schiffer Books
by the Author

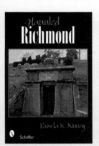

Haunted Richmond, Virginia. Pamela K. Kinney. Richmond names Edgar Allan Poe as its native son, and is rich in ghostly lore, legends, and tales. Learn why Virginia's governor shares his mansion with ghosts; dine with ghosts at Ruth's Chris Steak House and Crab Louie's Seafood Tavern; and read many interesting and scary stories!
Size: 6" x 9" • 24 b/w photos • 128 pp
ISBN: 978-0-7643-2712-4 • soft cover • $14.95

Haunted Richmond II. Pamela K. Kinney. Return once more to haunted Richmond. Step back in time at Henricus Historical Park, where you'll be welcomed by dead colonists, Civil War soldiers, and other haunts. Tour haunted hotels, churches, cemeteries, schools, and even a comic shop! No building is safe from the supernatural and Richmond's dead don't stay dead for long!
Size: 6" x 9" • 199 b&w images • 176 pp
ISBN: 978-0-7643-3964-6 • soft cover • $19.99

Haunted Virginia: Legends, Myths, and True Tales. Pamela K. Kinney. Like every state in the Union, Virginia has unique myths, legends, and yes, even true stories that sound much like legends, but aren't. Read Virginian stories of witches, demons, monsters, ghosts, pirates, strange animals, and soldiers from the Civil War. Come visit a most amazing, frightening, and even intriguing Virginia that you never knew existed.
Size: 6" x 9" • 45 b/w photos • 256 pp
ISBN: 978-0-7643-3281-4 • soft cover • $14.99

Virginia's Haunted Historic Triangle: Williamsburg, Yorktown, Jamestown, & Other Haunted Locations. Pamela K. Kinney. Hear odd noises and see apparitions at the Peyton Randolph House, Cornwallis's Cave, Wells's Corner, Sherwood Forest, the Rosewell Plantation, and many, many other places. Take a step back into the past and be prepared to get to know the ghosts of this Historic Triangle and its surrounding areas. They're dying for you to read their stories.
Size: 7" x 10" • 121 color images • 192 pp
ISBN: 978-0-7643-3746-8 • soft cover • $19.99

About the Author

Author of *Haunted Richmond, Haunted Richmond II, Haunted Virginia: Legends, Myths, and True Tales,* and *Virginia's Haunted Historic Triangle: Williamsburg, Yorktown, Jamestown, & Other Haunted Locations,* **Pamela K. Kinney** has written fiction that enables her readers to journey to worlds of fantasy, go beyond the stars, and dive into the vortex of terror. One of her stories proved heart-stopping enough to be runner up for 2013 WSFA Small Press Award. As Sapphire Phelan, she also writes bestselling paranormal romance with dark heroes and heroines with bite!